Little Girls Can Be Mean

Little Girls Can Be Mean

Four Steps to Bully-proof Girls in the Early Grades

Michelle Anthony, M.A., Ph.D., and
Reyna Lindert, Ph.D.

 St. Martin's Griffin ❦ New York

Library of Congress Cataloging-in-Publication Data

Anthony, Michelle.
    Little girls can be mean : four steps to bully-proof girls in the early
grades / Michelle Anthony and Renya Lindert.—1st ed.
          p.   cm.
    ISBN 978-0-312-61552-9
    1. Bullying in schools.   2. Girls—Violence against—United
States—Prevention.   3. Girls—Psychology.   4. Bullying.   I. Lindert,
Renya.   II. Title.
    LB3013.3.A58 2010
    371.5'8—dc22   2010012013

10   9

To Kylie, Maya, and Bryce:

It is through each of you that I have discovered so much about myself.
Thank you for taking me on the journey of a lifetime.

To Natasha, Nadia, and Carson:

May the lessons we continue to learn together help us to share, grow,
and better understand one another. It is our connection that has made
my discoveries and explorations possible.

To Scott and Nick:

whose love, guidance, and unwavering support allowed us to turn our
ideas into actions and our thoughts into *Little Girls Can Be Mean.*

To all the families who have shared their heartaches and
triumphs with us, and trusted we would carry on their power
and meaning with integrity in our work.

And to my brother, who showed me a miracle, and whose hidden
reserves of courage, strength, and determination have changed the way
I view hope and perseverance.

Contents

Contents

Contents

Acknowledgments

There are many people who made this endeavor possible. We extend great thanks to the families who have entrusted us with their stories and the professionals who have enlightened us with their talents: Emily and the McIllhenney family; Jenny and the Woo family; Ellen and the Regal/Hauk family; Sarah and the Schwarz family; Amber and the Etchieson family; Monica and the Kavalieros family; Hiroko and the Geddes family; Sam, Peter, and the Viner-Brown family; Kim and the Zwetchkenbaum family; Michael Thompson, Theresa McNally, and the Thompson family; Debbie Lienemann; Kristina Davies, Marisa Lovely; Cathi Long; Caroline Fields; Deirdre Marsters; Dana Hahn; Renee Cherneck; Jo-An Krivitsky; Sarah Sinclair; Erin Gettling; and the individuals and families we worked with who chose to remain anonymous. A special thanks goes to Paul Von Essen, who shared his knowledge and expertise over and over, and who let Michelle sit in on his bully-proofing classes time and again.

We owe a great deal of thanks to Alyse Diamond, for her

expertise in shaping (and shortening!) our work. We cannot fully express our appreciation to her for the degree to which she advocated for this project, and her instrumental role in helping us bring our vision of this guide to life. Thanks also to Kendra Marcus, for her attention to detail and the time and energy she put into helping us formalize our thoughts and present our ideas. We are truly grateful to Kathi Engelken, whose devotion to us as individuals and professionals has made this (and many other projects) possible.

Of course, we are deeply indebted to our families and friends for their steadfast belief in us and our work. Bonnie and Robert and Bruce and Barbara; Tricia and John, Max, and Will; Scott and Joanne, Charlie, and Holly; Michael and Jess, Luke, and Henry; Peter and David; Marc; Jeff; Ardith and Doug; Mark and Katherine, Owen, Sarah, and Malcolm; Chloe-Dog and Dee Dee; Roberta and Larry and Lin and Peter; Kathy and Sophie and Isabelle; Alex and Noemi and Alex; Jon and Elaine; Helen and Guillaume, Guilhem, and Claudia; Beryt; Wendy; Megan; Leslie; Cynthia; Marci; Terren; Laurie; Jennie; Helen; Dan; Laura; Elena; Yael; Amy; Wally, Dianna; Jean; Janet; Christa; Meghan; Jen; Joyce; Audrey; and Jennifer.

We could never have accomplished this project without the love and support of our children and spouses. It is through them that we understand deeply how these issues affect the families we are working to reach. They have been patient and loving as we continue along as imperfect guides and confidantes, and as a result, they have given us the greatest gift: the love, knowledge, and understanding of how friendship struggles shock and shape us, looking back and moving forward. We hope we can honor these lessons, and learn from them. And without Scott and Nick's loving encouragement and unfaltering belief in the importance of our work, neither of us could have begun—much less finished—this project. "Thank you" is not nearly enough.

Last, we wish to thank each of you—for opening your homes and your hearts to the Four-Step framework and for all the tips and strategies in *Little Girls Can Be Mean: Four Steps to Bully-proof Girls in the Early Grades*.

A Note to Readers

This book is not meant to replace professional support or guidance for you, your child, or any other individual. If you feel your daughter or another child is in danger, or is endangering another, you need to intervene and/or seek professional help immediately, regardless of the advice in this book. It is the responsibility of parents, teachers, counselors, and others to keep children safe, and if you have any concerns for the health, safety, or well-being of your child or those around her, act at once, without delay!

About the Authors

Michelle Anthony, M.A., Ph.D.

Dr. Michelle Anthony has always been passionate about her work with families and children. After graduating with honors in educational studies from Brown University, she went on to get her master's in child studies and her teacher's certificate from Tufts University. She taught in Massachusetts and Rhode Island for five years, after which she got her Ph.D. in developmental psychology from the University of California, Berkeley. Michelle has continued to work as a learning specialist with both typical and developmentally delayed preschool and elementary-aged students in both California and Colorado. She has taught graduate-level classes as well, and has been a speaker at various international conferences on issues related to education and development. Michelle is also a columnist and writes feature articles for Scholastic's *Parent and Child* magazine. She is the mother of three children, two girls and a boy, all under the age of nine.

As a result of her own daughter's involvement in a series of

Dr. Michelle Anthony and her three children: Maya, 5; Bryce, 2; and Kylie, 8.

"Mean Girl" interactions in first grade, Michelle's interest in this topic was personalized. She has since spent over three years interacting with counselors, social workers, school psychologists, teachers, principals, administrators, parents, and others around this topic—most of whom work within the Cherry Creek, Colorado, school district, where many feel bully-proofing programs began. She and her family live outside Denver, Colorado.

Reyna Lindert, Ph.D.

Dr. Reyna Lindert has always wanted and needed to work with young families in order to feel fulfilled personally and professionally. She is a certified parent educator with broad experience

Dr. Reyna Lindert and her three children: Natasha, 10; Carson, 3; and Nadia, 6.

working with elementary-aged children and their families. She graduated with distinction in human development and family studies from Cornell University. She then earned her M.A. and Ph.D. in developmental psychology from the University of California, Berkeley. Reyna is a skilled facilitator and has run interactive parenting workshops for families and children in California and Oregon. Reyna is also pursuing a degree in nursing at Oregon Health & Science University, to continue her work with young families in a health-care setting. She is the mother of three children, two girls and a boy, all under the age of eleven. They live outside Portland, Oregon.

Dr. Anthony and Dr. Lindert cofounded Wide-Eyed Learning, LLC, an organization devoted to facilitating communication and

I

Laying the Foundation:
The Four-Step Approach

The Rise of Social Cruelty

We have all heard the phrase before: Girls are mean—at least they can be. These words are said as a statement of fact and rarely questioned. It is the end of the discussion, as opposed to the beginning of one. Why is that? Why do we make no bones about stating that girls—indeed all children—can be openly and outwardly cruel, and yet we as parents, counselors, and educators feel so helpless to do anything about this? Cliques happen. Girls will be girls. Those girls we care about—be it our daughters, our clients, or our students—simply need to learn to navigate the rocky terrain of growing up female.

To a certain extent this is true. As long as there are groups of children who gather together in the minisociety we know as school, there will be wonderful acts of friendship and devastating acts of betrayal. The reality is that all children are capable of cruel acts: often as part of a group experience, sometimes on their own initiative. The longing to fit in and be part of something beyond themselves is not only a natural developmental drive but a necessary and even beneficial one. Our human need for connection is inherent, as is our need for food and water. The phrase "dying of loneliness" is as much a real possibility as it is a metaphor.

This powerful need to be part of a social group is firmly set by the time children enter elementary school. Even in preschool, children include or exclude one another; you've probably seen teasing, name-calling, and worse. Teachers will comfortably intervene at this age, mostly telling children they need to include everyone, be kind to their friends, or other such peacemaking instruction. But by elementary school, children are less supervised—even in kindergarten—and they begin to test the influence of their own power. They seek connections with friends at what might be described as "any cost."

Urban Anaya

Take Anaya*, a five-year-old African American kindergartener from an urban public school in Chicago. Anaya is described by her teachers as a bright, sweet girl. She is one of the "good kids" in the class, which means she is not a discipline problem in school. The twenty-eight children in Anaya's class come from a wide array of backgrounds—African American, Latino, Asian, Caucasian—and many are biracial. The teacher, Mrs. Hernandez, describes the group as one of her nicer classes. It is early in the

---

*Some names and identifying details have been changed to protect the privacy of the individuals and families involved.

year, but Mrs. Hernandez says there have not been many incidents that would raise the attention of the staff.

When asked what types of "incidents" she is referring to, Mrs. Hernandez is quick to list small offenses that will get a child a time-out or a loss of recess. She then goes on to name larger infractions that will result in a trip to the principal's office or a call to a child's parents. "There is the usual rough-and-tumble stuff. Boys who punch, pig piles that lead to bruises, stuff like that. A onetime event, as long as there is no blood or broken bones, we handle ourselves. But if we start noticing a pattern of aggressive behavior, or if a child or group of children is not able to learn some impulse control, we have to step up the discipline.

"We have zero tolerance for bullies at our school, and a strong anti-bully program. It's a six-week series that helps students identify and deal with bullying behaviors, when to get help, stuff like that. We've seen a real change in the ten years I've been teaching as a result. The principal is involved sooner. Parents are brought in. We take it all very seriously."

When asked which children are the ones who get in the kinds of trouble she describes, Mrs. Hernandez responds quickly, "Oh, it's far and away a boy problem. We certainly get our share of aggressive girls—you know, the ones who kiss the boys, pull hair, that kind of thing. But mostly, when you talk about the bigger-scale infractions, we have been dealing with boy aggression."

How does girl aggression manifest itself? Mrs. Hernandez has to think a moment. "Girl meanness. We have it at our school for sure, but mostly in the older grades. The cliques really begin in fourth grade, although you can see the prelude to them even in kindergarten. But it's not a problem like it is with the boys. With boys, kids can really get hurt."

Mrs. Hernandez's assessment is like many teachers', administrators', and parents': Girls can be mean. It's simply a fact of life. The sun shines, the rains come, and girls can be mean. They can exclude and betray, but it's the boys' physically aggressive behavior that can really lead to someone getting hurt. The truth of this statement at its surface is palpable—everyone longs to prevent school violence. Sadly, however, this belief system ignores a less physical, but potentially just as damaging, experience for half of the population.

Relational Aggression Research

The fact is, research has shown that girls can be just as aggressive as boys, if we redefine "aggressive acts" to include the verbal variety, like cruel words, the silent treatment, exclusion, backstabbing, rumor spreading, and other such behaviors. Social scientists who study friendship and group dynamics among children define such acts, including systematic teasing, as "relational aggression" or "social cruelty." Relational aggression is reported to be as painful to its victims as physical blows—and maybe more lasting in its effects.[1] Information from the Ophelia Project, a national nonprofit organization dedicated to addressing relational aggression in all its manifestations, states that relational aggression often results in physical symptoms, such as headaches or stomachaches, for both the aggressor and the target.[2]

Friendship struggles, relational aggression, and girl bullying clearly take their toll, and continue unaddressed, at least in part because of the fact that these behaviors are so "hidden" in girl culture that adults often don't even know they are happening. When they do, they frequently write them off. Researcher Nicki Crick, of the University of Minnesota, and her colleagues strongly disagree with this approach, defining relational aggression as "behaviors that harm others through damage (or the threat of damage) to relationships or feelings of acceptance, friendship, or group inclusion."[3]

Remembering Mrs. Hernandez's assessment of her kindergarteners, listen to Anaya nonchalantly relate a story that could be told on any playground at any school in any city or town: "In my kindergarten, at recess, there was a group of girls—the older ones—who were already six. There were also some of us who were still five, hanging out with them. Then one of them shouts out, 'Who is still only five?' The older girls only wanted to play with the six-year-olds, and I was still five. But I wanted to play with them, so I said I was six and they just believed me."

When asked why she told them she was six, she reports flatly, "It wasn't fair that they said you had to be six to play, and they were my friends so I wanted to play with them." And the other girls, the five-year-olds? "They were walking around us and they asked to play and the six-year-olds said, 'No! You can't play!' But I was glad I got to play." How did Anaya feel when she saw her five-year-old friends excluded? "I didn't care," she states matter-of-factly, "I was just glad that I could."

Is Anaya unusual in her desire to want to belong to the "in" club of the moment? Is she a "mean girl" for not thinking of the excluded girls? No, she is a normal, healthy, typical five-year-old girl trying to navigate the social waters of school life. Girls as young as three to five years of age exhibit patterns of relational aggression,[4] and these patterns have been found to be relatively consistent over time.[5] And Anaya (and her situation) are not unique to her or her school environment.

Private School Emma

Meet Emma, a kindergartener who attends a small, private K–8 school in a suburb of Boston. The school follows an established anti-bullying program and integrates lessons into every grade. Similar to Anaya, Emma is considered a good student, easygoing, and well liked.

Today Emma reports, "Rebecca is not my friend." When asked why, she responds, "Well, when I went up to her on the playground, she threw her arms in the air and shouted, 'Get away! Get away from me! I don't want to play with you! I'm playing with Lily!'" In Emma's reenactment we can see how startled she was at such a loud and demonstrative objection to something as "simple" as her wanting to enter the play. Teaching children how to join social interactions and make friends is a component of virtually every preschool and kindergarten in the country. Despite her school's inclusive policies, Rebecca felt no concern about openly (and vociferously) excluding another student. When asked what she did to confront the exclusion, Emma shrugs despondently. Did she remind Rebecca of the school's rules of inclusion? Was she able to get her other friend Lily to open the play to her? Did she run off to find friends who were more welcoming? "No," Emma tells us, looking downward, "I saw Rebecca whispering to Lily about me, so after that, I was alone."

Such scenarios are not unique to kindergarten. For many—if not most—girls, being included is of utmost importance, even at the price of "fairness" or other friendships, at least in that moment. Being excluded has a powerful impact on children. As is evident in Emma's response, the results may not be seen by the teacher, and they may not draw the attention of school personnel, but they significantly affect girls of all ages, socially and emotionally and, as you will also learn, academically. Even when retelling this story, Emma reexperiences the emotions she felt at the time of the incident. And she is not alone.

Friendship Struggles and Learning

Take Kayla, a friendly, outgoing eight-year-old from Stockton, California. Kayla walks into her second-grade class, excited to play with Hadley before the school day starts. The pair share laughs and touch each other's hair in a way that many young girls do as a show of affection. Mrs. Jackson calls the children over to the rug to begin Morning Meeting. When Mrs. Jackson is ready to talk about the calendar, it is clear that Kayla is not.

Kayla is distraught because her friend Sasha is being "mean." Kayla, Hadley, and Sasha can often be seen sifting rocks underneath the play structures, or taking turns on the monkey bars at recess, so Mrs. Jackson tries to uncover what has gone wrong in their friendship so early in the day. "Sasha told me that she didn't want to sit next to me on the rug."

Following up, Mrs. Jackson asks, "What did you do when she said that?"

"I came over to you," Kayla reports.

Mrs. Jackson tells her, "Well, you need to tell Sasha how that made you feel."

Kayla walks over to Sasha and says, "It made me really sad when you told me that I couldn't sit next to you."

"SHHH!" shouts Sasha, turning away. "I'm listening to Mrs. Jackson do the calendar!" Kayla, despondent, realizes that Mrs. Jackson has indeed begun Meeting. Not wanting to get in trouble or cause a scene, she sits down, her chin between her hands, eyes cast downward on the carpet.

As most parents and teachers will agree, every child—boy *and* girl—will have such experiences. However, research by developmentalists, educators, and psychologists shows that by adolescence, this systematic set of "female interactions" has taken its toll on girls' psyches and self-esteem.[6] These behaviors have also been associated with problems in peer relationships and with higher levels of depression.[7]

Hearing stories such as those of Anaya, Emma, and Kayla tells us why: Beginning in children's earliest days of mutual, sustained friendship—in fact, for almost the entirety of their social lives—girls are surrounded by or are participants in friendship struggles, relational aggression, and girl bullying. And the social cruelty ranges from everyday "benign" struggles to the "horror stories" that every parent longs to help her daughter avoid, such as being "defriended" or becoming a mean girl herself in order to stay tight with a group of girls. Increasing numbers of popular culture venues (for example, TV shows, magazine articles, and online communities)—as well as reports from countless parents in our parenting workshops—describe how Mean Girls are getting meaner, and suggest that the effects are being experienced at younger and younger ages.

Research has shown that the collection of such experiences over time can have a significant impact on a child's sense of self and her ability to learn.[8] Gary Ladd's Pathways Project is a long-term study of the various influences on children's early and continuing educational progress. This longitudinal study of children from kindergarten through middle school examines aspects of family and school that affect children's academic success. Results indicate that when children have difficulty with their peer group at school, they perform less well on measures of learning and achievement.[9]

Most Bully Programs "Miss the Mark"

Despite the blossoming of bully-proofing courses around the country, issues of girl meanness and female friendship struggles fall outside the scope of a majority of programs. Most address ways to manage and mitigate physical aggression, as opposed to friendship issues. For those that also discuss social cruelty, it is often the horror story types of relational aggression that are highlighted. In this way, the tools and strategies many schools emphasize relate more to male behaviors, or to acute acts of bullying.

"The schools' bully-proofing emphasis simply misses the mark for girls in the early grades," Penny, a mother of three girls, states flatly. "They do a good job talking about violence and obvious bullying, yet they almost completely ignore the catfights and social struggles of the girls. It's one thing to prepare yourself against the backstreet bully, but what do you do when the bully is your best friend?"

In reality, we know relatively little about the ways in which girls use relational aggression and social cruelty in the early elementary school years, or their impact. Yet it is the culmination of these early experiences that sets the stage for girl identity formation and the power (or lack thereof) that girls feel entering the stormy seas of middle school. Despite groundbreaking books such as *Reviving Ophelia, Best Friends, Worst Enemies,* and *Queen Bees and Wannabes,* very little has been written about how to help *young* girls problem solve and manage social relationships in the years *before* middle school.

However, the early elementary years provide a unique time in children's development: Girls are mature enough to begin entering the world independently, and yet parents, counselors, and educators remain strong figures of support. In contrast to the adolescent period, caring adults can more easily influence girls' social choices and responses to social cruelty and bullying. Through their guidance, adults can help shape girls' social development, if parents and their daughters are given an accessible plan and the appropriate tools and resources.

Having a way to recognize and address these issues early on is vital. It is during the early years that friendship struggles and relational aggression begin to dominate girl social dynamics. Not because girls are inherently mean, and not because girls are "more cruel" than boys. Children are participants in social interactions that are fostered (and often dictated) by group dynamics beyond the control of any one individual. The longing to belong is ingrained in all of us and remains part of our interactions into adulthood.

From our work with children in schools in Rhode Island, Massachusetts, New York, Oregon, California, and Colorado as teachers and parent educators, we have seen the power of social forces at work, especially for young girls. Like many educators, we have found that in order for teachers to teach subject matter, they need to learn how to recognize and respond to young girls' friendship issues. Often girls as young as kindergarten or first grade come to class distracted by a fight with a friend or some group social tension. They are so wrapped up in whatever is going on personally that they are not able to focus on learning.

In order to better participate in the classroom, girls need support in dealing with friendship struggles and social issues. Paul Von Essen is a social worker in the Cherry Creek School District in Littleton, Colorado, and a national speaker on bully-proofing. He explains, "We do bully-proofing so that teachers can teach and kids can learn." Having seen him work his magic with groups of young children, we know the power of this statement when it is backed by programs and action. Problems arise for girls, however, because the reality is that most bully-proofing programs ignore or gloss over the friendship struggles that affect girls' ability to learn at school.

Imagine the impact of a social system where young girls are often caught in what we call *yo-yo friendships*—relationships where a young girl's closest friend is often cruel or exclusionary one day, and again best friends with her the next, yo-yoing her back and forth and leaving her in a swirl of confusing emotions. So often girls are left alone to determine how to safely interact with peers.

They are supposed to figure out, on their own, how to let go of these hurts and fears so that they can focus on what they come to school to do—*to learn.*

Social Struggles Take Their Toll

While most children can easily move on from a single incident of teasing or exclusion on a given day, the accumulation of multiple incidents over days, weeks, months, and years will affect a girl's sense of self as a student, family member, and friend. Experiencing these events in virtually every facet of their lives—at recess, during math, in the hallways, and in music class—is affecting the ability of our girls to learn, participate, and lead even in elementary school. Sadly, friendship struggles, relational aggression, and girl bullying are glossed over because girls have had no language or framework to understand what is happening to them. They have not realized that such events warrant discussion, support, and, at times, intervention in order to be resolved.

Add to this the fact that the adults in their lives have similarly lacked language and a framework for these issues and therefore have not actively discussed them, problem solved around them, or intervened in them. It is no surprise, then, that young girls have felt so alone in their social troubles. Talia, an articulate eleven-year-old from Berkeley, California, explains, "Even if you try and tell the other girls to include you, they will just laugh. So you can go and tell a teacher, but the teacher just says, 'Find someone else to play with.' Teachers don't like to walk over to the girls and tell them they have to be fair or nice or whatever. That's what happens at my school. I always feel sad and mad about it—that the teachers don't notice what is going on, and even if they did, they wouldn't help. They don't think it is a real problem at all."

Of course, there are many sympathetic educators who understand exactly what their female students are going through. However, they, like the girls' parents, lack the overarching understanding of how these issues affect girls' social development and ability to learn. Or they lack the resources and strategies to successfully problem solve with and support their young students, especially within the confines and limits of their roles as teacher and advocate for *each* child under their care.

Friendship struggles, relational aggression, and girl bullying affect most, if not all, girls—including those from affluent backgrounds, or those deemed "popular." And the "everyday" tales related in this chapter are simply the tip of the iceberg. Over the course of this book, you will hear from many other girls in the early grades whose stories have stunned and shaped them, but through whom you can apply a new framework to approach social issues in a systematic fashion.

Parents and sympathetic educators feel at a loss for how to understand, much less interact with and support, their young daughters or students as they begin to navigate the waters of friendship and group dynamics. Parents in particular are often confused. They may feel relief (and a new sense of freedom) that their girls are finally independent enough to not "need" them in the intense and often draining way that babies and preschoolers need their parents. Their daughters can now go to birthday parties and playdates alone, have friendships that are free of constant parental mediation, and are able to participate in self-selected activities with more independence. At the same time, parents are surprised by the unexpected and complicated "clique-y" issues that surface in early elementary school—conflicts they don't expect to see until their girls are older, more mature, and better able to handle them. They are caught off guard by the fact that their daughters seem so unready or unable to row the waters alone. To make matters worse, parents themselves feel ill-equipped to help their children steer.

It is within these currents that *Little Girls Can Be Mean: Four Steps to Bully-proof Girls in the Early Grades* was born. Similar in philosophy to our other work with young children, *Little Girls Can Be Mean* is driven by the belief that children learn best in meaningful interactions with those they trust—their parents, caregivers, counselors, and educators. Through the Four-Step plan we have developed, you will learn how to approach girl social struggles in a step-by-step fashion. You will learn intuitive, effective strategies to help the girls you love not only put words to the struggles they face in these early school years but also develop a *plan of action* when challenged with inevitable conflict or betrayal. Different from a list of good ideas or a disparate array of possible suggestions, *a logical, ordered, explicit* plan will make a world of difference in your child's ability to approach and handle tough issues. In *Little Girls Can Be Mean*, we give you a *specific Four-Step plan* that will enable you to support your daughter as she faces a host of different types of friendship issues, social cruelty, and bullying situations in the coming years.

As detailed in the coming chapters, you will learn how to *observe* (Step 1), *connect* (Step 2), *guide* (Step 3), and *support your girls to act* (Step 4) in various social circumstances. Drawing on this new framework, you will become a problem-solving partner with the child you love. You will be able to provide girls of all ages with new tools that they can use on their own to confront social struggles. *Little Girls Can Be Mean* is written with every girl in mind: shy, outgoing, athletic, studious, dramatic, free-spirited, a combination of these, or somewhere in between. The book will build strong bonds of support between parents and daughters, between counselors and clients, and between teachers and students in the window of time *before* children begin to shut caring adults out—before cliques and best friends push adults away. Furthermore, the book gives girls themselves the ability to make active, empowered choices from a very young age.

Little Girls Can Be Mean is a guide for parents, counselors, and educators of young girls, girls who are—by virtue of their age—mature enough to (begin to) reason, weigh, plan, respond, enact, and review, but still young enough to comfortably challenge themselves to change, take risks, bare their souls, and open their hearts. *Little Girls Can Be Mean* uses interactive activities and true stories to demystify the social world of girls aged five to twelve (kindergarten through sixth grade). Perhaps more importantly, the Four-Step plan will give caring adults and the girls they love an easy-to-understand, productive way to respond to the inevitable struggles every girl faces as she enters (and sometimes gets excluded by) the world of groups, clubs, and best friends. In doing so, we give parents and teachers the tools to buoy children up, to stand up to and deal with social cruelty rather than face the impossible task of doing away with the cruelty.

TEACHER'S Tip

We work through the Four-Step plan from the perspective of a parent; however, the strategies are just as relevant for teachers, counselors, and other professionals. Additional strategies specifically for professionals will appear throughout, in boxes like this one.

Throughout the book you will notice that we write with a common voice, sharing our training and expertise as developmental psychologists, researchers, educators, and parenting experts. At various points, we also share our experiences as parents just like you, in addition to the stories from our ambassador children. We bring these experiences to you as mothers to six young children—each of us with two girls and a boy. Michelle's children, Kylie, Maya, and Bryce, are eight, five, and two; Reyna's children, Natasha, Nadia, and Carson, are ten, five, and two. They have bravely agreed to share some of their own stories with you in hopes that some of their struggles and triumphs will make a difference in the lives of your own families.

Tip for Girls: Create a Journal

Parents, these boxes are meant specifically for girls themselves, and in them, we speak directly to your daughters, sharing strategies, activities, and ideas. Of course, you can also choose to read them to your daughter or talk about the activities with her. Show your daughter these boxes, inviting her to become involved in this journey more fully!

Hey, girls! Have your parents look for these boxes throughout the book. They have ideas, information, and activities meant just for you, to think about or do on your own or with the support of caring adults. Create a lasting connection by sharing any of them with your parents!

To help you get started, let's make a safe space to think, draw, and write. So get yourself a notebook or journal that feels special, or that you can make special. Not only will this give you some private space to organize your thoughts, but it is a great way to allow yourself to look back a few months from now, to see how your thinking has grown or changed. Decorate the book (the outside, the inside, or both!). Look through magazines, get photos or clip art from the computer, or draw items yourself. Make pictures of things you love to do, things that make you feel great about yourself. Things that cheer you up or make you laugh. Anything you want. It's your book. Make it beautiful in its own way.

In addition to the "Tips for Teachers" and the "Tips for Girls" boxes, the "Think, Share, Do . . ." chapters of the book are full of questions and age-appropriate suggested activities. Consider which questions, stories, or activities are best suited to the personalities of the girls you care for or work with, or the situations that they are facing or have dealt with. But don't forget to stretch yourselves and try an activity you may not have thought of—you may be delighted with what you discover! The questions and activities are based on the Four Steps and are designed to be revisited again and again, over the next handful of years—as your child develops, matures, or faces new conflicts with different sets of skills. You will find that the activities lend themselves to reaching both younger and older girls, depending on the level of support you provide. If you have more than one daughter or work with multiple girls, you will likely find that each girl responds differently, and each will take you on a different journey at different points in development.

The activities are not meant for girls to do alone, although they could. Similarly, activities, exercises, and scenarios are not meant to be worked through quickly. Rather, they are structured to invite you to spend time talking, listening, and problem solving *together*. Let your own conversations grow from those in this book, and emphasize the importance of your daughter's, client's, or student's own stories over any that may be suggested within these pages.

In the following chapter, we lay out the Four-Step plan for standing up to, dealing with, and resolving girl friendship struggles, relational aggression, and bullying in the early years. In the context of the Four Steps, you will learn a variety of *tools and strategies* that will help the girls you love deal with the complex world of being female.

Part I concludes with chapter 3, the "Think, Share, Do . . . Activity Bank," through which you can begin using the Four-Step plan in your interactions with your daughter(s), client(s), or student(s). The discussions, activities, and guided observations will build a strong foundation of connection between you and your child. From there, the two of you will be able to confront the myriad social dilemmas that are likely on the horizon, or that she is presently contending with. You will want to visit this section *as* you read the accompanying chapters, as opposed to only happening upon it at the end.

We follow with Part II, "The Heart of the Matter: Applying the

Four Steps to Real Situations Faced by Real Girls." In each of the three chapters in this part, you will hear real stories from girls and parents in their own words. We then briefly explain what happened and why, to emphasize the developmental framework that situations such as these occur in. This allows you not only a glimpse of your child's social world but also a better appreciation of the universal experience of friendship struggles. From there, we identify what the child did well in the circumstances at hand, to help you recognize that your daughter comes to these situations with skills that just need refining. Then, in each scenario, we show you how to apply the Four-Step plan—we walk you through how to observe, connect, guide, and support your girls to act. In so doing, we use each story to help you identify all-purpose strategies that you can use in your own life, regardless of how your individual situation may differ from that described.

The stories in Part II were chosen because they highlight universal struggles confronted by five- to twelve-year-old girls. In applying the Four-Step plan to these stories, you will find strategies that work with the most frequent issues that arise in girl friendships.

Chapter 4, "Side by Side: Best Friends, Worst Enemies," covers what can go wrong within pairs of girls, and how to address these challenges. Using the Four Steps, you will learn how to handle situations such as when one girl breaks away from a friendship in a hurtful way, or when your daughter is trapped in a yo-yo relationship and is suffering through an unrelenting hot/cold cycle of a loving-and-abusive friendship.

In chapter 5, "Going Along with the Gang," you will learn to help girls contend with group dynamics and friendship circles.

These issues include having friends pressure your daughter to go against what is comfortable for her in order to stay a member of the group, or when girls exclude a member of their friendship circle for being "different," among others. As with all the chapters in this section, how to problem solve using the Four-Step plan is the focus.

Chapter 6, "All Girls Can Be Mean: When Your Daughter Is Acting Like a Mean Girl," begins with anecdotes from parents about times they've perceived that their daughters are acting mean. Through the Four Steps, we better understand where Mean Girl behavior comes from, and how parents can shape it so that girls can be assertive and strong while remaining kind and well liked by their peers.

In chapter 7, we extend the "Think, Share, Do . . . Activity Bank." Within these pages you will find activities and discussion questions you can return to again and again over the next handful of years that will advance your thinking, enhance your connection with the girls you care about, and extend your understanding of the social situations faced by the girls you love. You can take advantage of any activity at any time.

The final chapter of the book, "Wrapping Up: Using the Four Steps in Your Home, School, or Office," looks at the developmental change girls experience over the elementary school years. This knowledge will help you take the tools you have learned in the book and apply them to your own life, as the girls you work with and love grow and change.

With the structure and guidance of the Four Step Plan, you and the girls you care about will have a wonderful opportunity to solidify a partnership at a crucial point in development. While this book may not stop the tears and anguish of friendship lost or betrayed, we can help you help your daughter, client, or student better understand herself and the girls around her, giving her the tools and the strength to draw on as she more fully enters the world of being female.

Don't forget to take advantage of the activities and discussion questions in the "Think, Share, Do . . . Activity Bank for Part 1" on page 54. You will want to visit these pages often, to take full advantage of how the Four-Step process can enhance your relationship and support you and the girls you care for or work with.

2

How Can I Help My Daughter
or Student?

This much is certain: All girls will face their fair share of social conflict and struggle at various points along the way to maturity. Much as we might wish it were different, there is no way to fully protect the girls we care about from the pain and heartache they experience as they find their way in the world. So what can we—their devoted parents, caregivers, teachers, and counselors—do to support them and to help alleviate the pain of growing up? The answer is twofold: we can work to *prevent* social struggles, relational aggression, and girl bullying, and we can *respond to and mitigate* their pervasive effects. Taking advantage of the Four-Step plan helps us to do both, simultaneously.

So often, parents look at each difficulty as a new and separate problem. In actuality, the individual problems are merely symptoms of a bigger issue below the surface. When you have a better sense of how your child functions—what contributes to her successes and struggles—you will be able to support her in addressing both the overarching and the underlying issues. To do this, you need a systematic way to help your child every time she experiences conflict, so that you are not constantly in the position of shooting from the hip. One of the many benefits of the Four-Step plan is that it takes all the guesswork out of having to wonder and worry about how much to step back and how much to step in! Simply follow the steps for each social struggle your child faces, and let your discoveries from each piece of the process inform how you follow through on the next.

Along the way, you will come to understand the underlying issues that drive your child's choices, which will help you to further support her in the decisions she must make as an independent individual navigating her way through the world. You'll no longer have to address these issues on the fly in a haphazard fashion. Instead, you are the knowledgeable and approachable guide who is prepared to support your child through any struggle she is facing (or will face) using an organized, responsive, coherent Plan.

If you feel your daughter or another child is in danger, or is endangering another, you need to take action and seek professional help immediately, regardless of the advice in this book. It is the responsibility of parents, teachers, and counselors to keep the children in their care safe, and if you have any concerns for the health, safety, or well-being of your child or those around her, act at once, without delay. Your child's (or another child's) health and well-being should always be of paramount concern.

What Is Bullying?

Bullying usually occurs on a wide spectrum, which makes it difficult to offer a precise definition. At one end of the spectrum are children's *unintentionally* mean acts. In the course of trying to find themselves or assert their own social power, kids often act meanly or make unkind, "bullying" choices. At the other end of the spectrum are acts of clear-cut, intentional cruelty. Because girls are capable of both kinds of acts, and because girls are damaged by

---

Tip for Girls: What Is a Bully?

In this book, we talk to your parents about friendship struggles and bullying. Even nice girls can sometimes *act* like bullies. That is part of why talking about and understanding bullies is hard—because often girls who are our friends can *also* bully us, even if it is not all the time (sometimes it's even by accident!). So it can feel hard to know what is just a onetime mean act done by accident, and what is "really" bullying. The truth is, how you define these things doesn't matter. If what is going on is making you sad, making it hard to learn in school, or otherwise making life hard, we want you to get support! But in order to do that, you yourself need to feel like a situation is worth talking about with your parents or other trusted adults, to let them also guide your thinking!

- Some bully behaviors are obvious. List four and share with your mom or dad
- Some bully behaviors are less obvious. List four and share with your mom or dad

---

both kinds of acts (and everything in between), we do not split hairs over whether some acts are "true bullying" while others are not. We consider both types to be worthy of addressing.

Paul Von Essen, the social worker in the Cherry Creek School District in Littleton, Colorado, and national speaker on bully-proofing whom we introduced in chapter 1, believes that the actions of children in younger grades (K–2) more often fall on the "unintentionally mean" end of the bullying continuum. These children are just figuring out how to "be somebody" in the social scene, and their mean acts are not done with the intention of hurting others so much as with the desire to assert themselves, albeit ineffectively. Children at this age are somewhat egocentric and can neither preview nor immediately realize the effect their actions have on others, and thus the *intent* to hurt is usually absent.

The actions of girls in grades 3 and up, on the other hand, can span the entire continuum. And, as children get older, they will witness (and, for some, participate in) an increasing number of actions at the more overt end of the bullying spectrum. Starting in third grade, girls get more socially sophisticated and true cliques begin to form. In addition, you see actions with the intent to hurt others occur more frequently, with most participants realizing (at least to some degree) how their choices are influencing others.

Regardless of how old your child is, and regardless of whether other children are intending to do harm, if your child is suffering socially, we feel it is appropriate to take advantage of the Four Steps to protect and support her.* If she is trying to assert

---

*For readability, we say "daughter" and "your child" from here on; however, teachers and counselors should substitute "student" or "client," as the Four-Step framework is

her power and gain some control and does so in inappropriate or hurtful ways, the Four Steps will also guide you in how to respond to and support her.

Building the Foundation

Before your child is entangled in serious social strife, we encourage you to take advantage of the activities in this guide and reflect on the real situations girls like yours have faced (see Part II). Doing so will give you the opportunity to support your child to develop general skills and strategies that will guide her in everyday social interactions before those interactions turn ugly. You will also give her the strength and experience to navigate these typical situations before they get complicated. And, importantly, you will enhance and strengthen the relationship the two of you share. It is the strength and stability of this relationship that we return to again and again throughout these pages, to help you help your child. Even if your child is "only" in kindergarten, even if she is "already" in sixth grade, or even if she has yet to face (to your knowledge) any truly sticky social situations, we encourage you to take advantage of the Four-Step framework.

Of course, while taking advantage of the Four-Step plan early on will help your child build a solid foundation of social power, *you can't control the other children who are also involved in what can*

---

equally relevant in school or other settings. In addition, most of the strategies and activities are equally effective for educators, caregivers, and counselors, and the girls with whom they work. For additional strategies and activities specific to the school environment, look for Teacher's Tip boxes.

become high-stakes situations. The friendship skills your child is developing will be tested; she will be pushed by her peers to execute newly established skills when she is simultaneously hurt, embarrassed, angry, and otherwise put on the spot.

In some ways, you are faced with a choice: In the words of Paul Von Essen, social worker and national speaker on bully-proofing, you can try to *spare* your child the natural struggles in life, by trying to (over)protect her from every little thing, or you can work to *prepare* her for them. One way to best prepare her is by using the Four-Step plan to learn who your child is as a problem solver. Then, work together to face life's inevitable challenges. While it might be nice to think you can spare your child from life's struggles, you serve her better when you *prepare* her. The goal in doing so is not to fix the problem *for* your daughter, but rather *to help her develop the skills she needs to fix her own problems.*

Facing Tough Situations

Until your child is faced with social struggles, you (and she!) often won't know she lacks the skills needed for a specific situation. Thus, while there is no doubt that building general social skills will help your child fare better socially, you and she will need to take what you learn within these pages and apply it to *specific* situations—situations neither of you can fathom at this point in time. If you think about it, how could Anaya's parents or teachers predict that the girls in her class would announce a "six-year-olds-only" club? Or that Emma's friend Lily would feel too underconfident to challenge Rebecca when she broke the school rule and actively excluded Emma from the play?

If you picked up this book because your daughter is *presently* facing difficult social situations, the Four-Step plan can help you help her to respond to and mitigate the pervasive effects of relational aggression, social power plays, and bullying. No doubt you are eager to flip through the pages and begin applying the suggestions right away. We, too, want the suggestions and strategies in this book to be immediately useful and easily applied, and we developed them with that in mind. However, be aware that there is logic to the order suggested for each of the Steps. In order to maximize what *Little Girls Can Be Mean* has to offer, you will want to follow *each* Step, and to do so in the suggested order. Skipping Steps, or shortchanging the suggested process involved, will not save you any time in the long run. Don't forget to also read additional chapters and strategies as the sense of urgency regarding the immediate issue subsides—to build a foundation of skills and support for the next, yet-unseen struggle looming on the horizon.

Following the Four-Step Plan

Often, children feel paralyzed and overwhelmed by social struggles that they worry adults will see as unimportant. As a result, they keep their feelings of sadness or worry to themselves for too long. The goal of the Four-Step plan is to establish a wonderful two-way relationship between you and your daughter, which will then give the two of you the means to face social struggles as a team. Our approach will enable you to observe the need for interaction and then establish a connection of support and understanding. From there, you will provide guidance to create new understanding and a set of possible choices, which will leave you ready to support her to act on her own behalf.

As we have emphasized, the Four-Step plan that follows can (and indeed should!) be used preemptively, *in addition to* being applied to the social conflicts your daughter is presently facing. What this may look like in different scenarios girls this age tend to face is described in great detail in the coming chapters, where we emphasize common themes and strategies across a variety of scenarios. For instance, Amelia's story (see page 126) involves worrying which socks to wear for Crazy Sock Day. On a more general scale, this scenario really highlights the struggle girls go through when they are trying to fit in to school culture. Thus, the suggestions apply to scenarios where girls are panicked about doing "it" (whatever "it" is) just right.

Each of the stories in this book has been selected for its more universal application to the many types of concerns girls in grades K–6 experience. For this reason, you will want to read each of the scenarios, keeping in mind its more widespread application. While you will find that some of the stories involve peer struggles and social power plays (on the more subtle end of the bullying continuum), there are also those that are quite overt. Make no mistake: Each kind of bullying is devastating to the girl trapped within it.

Below we introduce you to the Four Steps, we will describe them in general terms, and include several overarching strategies that we will draw on repeatedly throughout this guide.

Step 1: Observe

The seemingly simplest of the Steps, *observe*, is actually a multi-faceted skill. On the one hand, it is exactly as it sounds—look around and literally see what is going on in front of you. On the other hand, the power and importance of observing is so great that you will use this skill in a variety of settings, and throughout the Four-Step process, as we explain below.

Observing before social struggles occur

One of the best ways to know, especially on an intuitive level, if your daughter is struggling socially is to watch how she interacts with her friends on the playground or on a playdate, in order to assess her social skills or see how the friendship is getting along.

Observing also requires listening with an attentive ear to your daughter's choice of words and overall affect as she kicks around a soccer ball or puts together art projects at the kitchen table with her friend. And, of course, you will also want to be watching and listening when your child happily tells stories about friends and recess games. When the inevitable social struggle occurs, you will have a point of comparison when something about your child's tone, facial expression, and word choice seems "off," compared to her usual demeanor.

Observing when your child comes to you directly

Observing is vitally important even if your child comes to you directly and says, "I need to talk about what happened today." In this situation, take a moment to observe the bigger picture: Have there been any cues that something like this was building? Have you noticed any changes in behavior that would have indicated something else was going on in your child's life? Also take a moment to observe your child as she tells her story: Is she more angry, scared, sad, or embarrassed than usual? Is she displaying any nervous habits such as hair twirling or nail biting? Taking a moment to observe even when it seems like you don't have to (your child is standing there ready to share a social struggle with you, after all!) will put you in a far better place for the moments when your observations will be key. These are times when, for whatever reason, the particular problem your child is struggling with is so big, confusing, or embarrassing that in that instance she is incapable of coming to you.

Observing when your daughter doesn't come to you directly

Trust your instincts. Parents are often able to sense that something is not quite right, even without their daughter saying a word. Be conscious about observing subtle indicators of child stress—indicators that something is amiss or that your child needs support. For instance, you may notice changes in sibling interactions, in family behaviors, or in her moods. You may hear your daughter make very generalized complaints about school, teachers, or friends and use certain buzzwords like "mean," "unfair," or "bossy" that may point to hidden messages contained in seemingly benign stories. You may also notice a decreased level of excitement about activities she used to enjoy.

In these cases, observing is the ability to "hear" what your child has not yet directly told you. You can investigate a bit—is she having an off day? Is she overtired? Are there other factors that might explain the change in behavior? If not, and possibly even so, having this level of information will help you to better navigate the next three Steps: connecting, guiding, and supporting to act.

Observing and the next three Steps

As we mentioned earlier, observing is so important that it is also an active component of the next three Steps. Thus, in the sections that follow, we return to this skill to help you see how it plays out throughout the Four-Step process. Please know that observing is meant to be quick and simple—a way of checking in before you move on to the next step.

Step 2: Connect

Once you know (or suspect) that there is something going on with your child, your instinct may be to step in, determine what is wrong, and try to fix the problem, especially if your daughter is younger. And while there is nothing inherently wrong with this desire, in the long run, doing so will disempower your daughter. Instead, connecting with your child (Step 2) regardless of her age and empowering *her* to make active, informed decisions will help you and her build the strongest possible foundation from which to tackle social issues for the next decade and beyond.

Connecting before social struggles occur

The best time to fortify your relationship with your child is before any tension or social difficulties arise. Regardless of how strong your relationship has been, as children become more independent and capable, you'll likely find yourself correcting, directing, and (strongly) suggesting with greater frequency. If you also have younger children to take care of, it is common to want your older child to help out more and show more independence and competence. While this is natural and often necessary, it is also valuable to take a step back and find the time to simply connect with your child, without an end goal in mind. Many of the activities in this book will help you do just that.

Think about replacing your standard "How was your day?" or "What did you learn at school today?" with some socially focused questions. Reyna found that she learned far more about Natasha's friends when she specifically asked whom she played with on the playground, if she sat next to any new friends, or which girls were best friends on any given day. As parents with busy lives and multiple responsibilities, we know it is not possible to engage in these kinds of interactions all the time. However, even if you

TEACHER'S Tip: Create a "Caring Community"

Connect with students by creating a "Caring Community" from the first day of school. Reyna's daughter Natasha had a third-grade teacher who was skilled at creating a supportive classroom community. She invited the children to do "popcorn appreciations" (the children offered their thoughts spontaneously without waiting to be called on) at the end of each day's "community circle." For example, the students would say, "I appreciate Sarah because she played with me at recess today/helped me on my project/etc." When the teacher noticed some students not being spontaneously appreciated, she would either show appreciation for these children herself or say, "Look around and notice who hasn't been mentioned yet today. Who is ready to appreciate those classmates?"

only do it for periods of time and then let it lapse for a while, you will see the difference in your relationship.

Active listening

Connecting with your child and seeing the world from her perspective is a vital step toward helping her articulate her own experience (and solve her own problems). There are a great many ways you can connect with your child, and these will be expanded on throughout this book. One strategy you will see us return to often is *Active Listening*. Active Listening is a way of remaining fully attentive to your child, without imparting your feelings, values, or judgments. It is a way of reflecting back the heart of your daughter's thoughts or feelings in order to encourage her to further clarify her own thinking. Doing so also helps you to focus on fully *understanding* your child, instead of trying to fix, explain, or intercede.

To take advantage of Active Listening, restate a condensed version of what you have heard your child say. This will help you to "check in" to make sure if you've correctly understood your child's basic message. As you listen to her speak, ask yourself: "What is my daughter *thinking* or *feeling,* and what is she really trying to tell me?" Dig through the details and determine your daughter's main message *without adding your judgments or introducing new ideas.* Doing so will help you to connect with your child and help her better understand what is making her feel stressed or overwhelmed.

Active listening statements

"It sounds like you were angry that Jenna did not save you a seat on the bus."

"You're worried that Mr. Ashad will blame you for the misplaced work."

"Hmmm . . . that's a lot of information. Let me see if I understand. You are worried that Sarah is becoming best friends with Lizzie, and that will leave you with no one to play with at recess, is that right?"

"Wow! There's a lot going on there. I can see why you would feel confused. Let me see if I am understanding. You and Maggie decided to play hopscotch all week. But yesterday she said she was bored with that game. Today it seemed like she wanted to play hopscotch, but not with you. You are feeling sad and worried that your friendship with Maggie might be over. Have I understood you correctly?"

Notice that all of the above comments are forms of restating what your child is thinking or feeling, without your judgment or guidance.

The end goal of Active Listening is to connect in an empathetic way with your child. The following examples of empathetic statements should help guide you:

"I can imagine feeling lonely, sitting on the bus by myself. Were you nervous the rest of the day would be like that at school?"

"I know how important it is to you to be responsible. It must have been hard to feel unable to tell Mr. Ashad what really happened."

"You have been a loyal friend to Sarah. I can imagine feeling worried about needing to maybe find new friends to play with. How are you feeling about it?"

"Wow. I can understand you being disappointed in Maggie for backing out of your agreement and walking away from your friendship. I can imagine feeling really sad, and maybe a little angry."

Consider if you had tacked on a statement like, "Let's find another friend to play hopscotch with." Then you would have jumped prematurely into problem solving *for your daughter.* Instead of sorting out her own feelings, she would have to agree to move on or to resist choosing another friend. You would have lost your moment of connection and shortchanged her ability to better understand her own emotions and reactions because you tried to solve the problem too quickly.

Keeping the emphasis on your daughter's emotions *gives power back to your child.* She can agree or disagree with what you understood, but you (and she) should still be focused squarely on her and her experience. With better understanding of how she feels about the situation, she will be ready to then move on, consider multiple perspectives, and plan a course of action for herself. As counterintuitive as it may seem, taking the time to connect actually *increases* your effectiveness as an advocate and support to your daughter, and it *shortens* the time needed to move into effective guiding and acting. Remember, the length of the conversation is not what determines the strength of your connection. In fact, some connections will be nothing more than a quick comment or a simple discussion on the ride home from school or in passing at dinner. Think quality, not quantity.

In the words of Philip Stanhope, Fourth Earl of Chesterfield, "Many a man [sic] would rather you heard his story than grant his request." Looking at this through the eyes of your daughter, being heard and understood is one of the most important things you can do. Social struggles will come and go. But the connection you and your child forge in the process—the way you solidify yourselves as a team—will remain with you both for years and will strengthen your relationship. The coming chapters highlight numerous ways to connect with your child as she faces social struggles and girl bullying. This is the second step in the Four-Step process.

Observe while connecting

Part of connecting with your child also involves observing. This is a more focused observation than what we described above—it is specifically focused on noticing your daughter's reactions to your attempts to connect with her. That is, at various points along the way—even if you and she have a wonderfully strong relationship—your daughter may put up unconscious roadblocks when you try to connect with her. This may be because the situation feels so overwhelming, because she feels so vulnerable, because she is overcome with emotions, or simply because she is growing and changing and it is hard to feel unskilled and unprepared.

If you are able to observe some of her responses to your attempts to connect, you will likely reach her sooner, and be in a better position to guide and support her to act. So rather than get defensive if things are not clicking the way you wish (or think) they should, take a moment to observe: Is she a giggler? Does she get serious? Does it stress her out to talk about these issues? Noticing her reactions will give you valuable information in terms of learning how to approach her in times of struggle, as well as letting you know how she may subtly initiate communicating that struggles are occurring. For instance, you might notice that your daughter often says, "It's no big deal" as a way of saying, "I'm uncomfortable and embarrassed, but I still need support."

Step 3: Guide

Once you have observed a situation (or a notable change in your child) and connected with your daughter as you determine what might be going on, you are ready guide her (Step 3). When you guide your child, you work *together* to allow *her* to better understand the situation and to come up with a wide array of possibilities, any combination of which the two of you together can decide to help her to explore. As you guide her, you have the opportunity as the knowledgeable adult to support your child. Some common themes you will see us return to time and again are:

- ❖ Identifying the real issue, which may or may not be the problem she first mentioned, or the problem she is telling you
- ❖ Depersonalizing the situation and presenting alternative perspectives
- ❖ Scaling the worry down (or up) to size
- ❖ Brainstorming a number of possibilities
- ❖ Helping her understand the dynamics of her friendship group, her place within it, how she feels about that, and

how best to respond to her new knowledge. You can begin these discussions as young as kindergarten, but her ability to integrate this information into decision making will develop over the next few years

This is not to say your daughter will instantly see the situation from another viewpoint, that she will quickly identify the true issue (as opposed to the surface one she is currently in a panic over), or that she will immediately feel that the brainstormed suggestions are doable. But the mere act of seeing that there are numerous *possible* solutions to a seemingly impossible problem is empowering for your child. Encouraging her to contribute to the brainstorming session will also give her an increased sense of her own power (in the end). Be aware of the role you are committing to when you guide your child. For instance, if you decide together that increasing the number of playdates she has with individual friends might be beneficial, you need to be prepared to help follow through on this. Only leave items on the final list that are truly possible for you both to see through.

Guiding before social struggles occur

You will help your child immensely if you build a relationship that gives you the opportunity to guide her before social conflicts begin. You might do this by helping her extend a skill set she already possesses (for example, reaching out to friends in her class for playdates) or one that she is working on (meeting new friends). You might also think about guiding her in areas outside of the social arena (balancing homework with after-school activities, for example).

If you choose to support her organizational skills, for example, you would first observe how her disorganization affects her at home or in relation to school. In connecting with her, you would listen to what is hard for her about getting or keeping organized. Without judgment, you would reflect back what you hear as she talks about what it feels like to arrive at school without her homework, or to not be able to find her favorite sweatshirt. From there you would guide her, helping her see herself as powerful within this situation; working together to brainstorm some ways

TEACHER'S Tip: Before Social Struggles Begin

Creating a Caring Community before social struggles start in your classroom will help the school year move along more smoothly. At the beginning of each quarter:

1. Tell or remind children of the roles they can play at school to help create a Caring Community. Some ideas: *friend, helper, sharer, includer, encourager, risk taker.*

2. Give examples of how children can meet these expectations, with explanations in words or by showing kids in action with photos.

3. Observe (and comment on!) behaviors every chance you get. Tell your class that they will be able to point out these Caring Community behaviors at the end-of-the-day meeting. Building on the concept of "popcorn appreciation," students can say, "I noticed that Jane was a supporter today, when she told Sarah what a good job she did on the math quiz."

Remember, kids often do what works, not what is right or best. Your job is to make the *right* thing be what works in your classroom.

for her to be better organized. Remember, this is not the time for you to flat-out tell her what you want her to do to be better organized. Following the Four Steps means *she has a vital role* in brainstorming and in deciding what it is she is ready to take on or change when you move on to Step 4—support to act.

Sharing Stories

One powerful way for you to guide your daughter is to take advantage of a strategy we call Sharing Stories. By telling her a story from your own life that mirrors her experience, you make a connection with her through common ground. Thus, if your daughter comes to you distraught about her friend not speaking to her, connect with her, and then you may choose to confide in her that a similar situation happened when you were younger. Your daughter will be eager to hear that she is not alone in facing social setbacks and disappointments.

TEACHER'S Tip: Sharing Stories

Open the door to communication by telling a student, "One time I had a student who faced the same issue as you are facing right now." If she feels less alone, she will be more ready for guidance.

Observe while guiding

While guiding, observing means that you are noticing whether or not your child is *participating*. *Notice* if she gets distracted as you plan out ways to support her, suggesting that your guidance may be overwhelming or otherwise hard to digest. The end goal of Step 3 is to encourage her to feel that *she* is capable of choosing some strategies to implement. Observing in these moments may help you realize that you need to forge a stronger connection, to allow her to feel that you are a team working *together,* before you write down your next great idea. This is the power of observing along the way!

Step 4: Support to Act

The previous three Steps have been in service to this final one: Supporting your child to act from a secure base (your relationship) and a place of personal power. The goal here is to engage in a dialogue about the pros and cons of various possible actions, some of which will involve others (for example, sending a letter) and some of which will be done alone by your daughter or with you to support (for example, practicing in front of a mirror). How your child chooses to take action in dealing with friendship struggles will

---

Tips for Girls: Furthering Friendship Through Letter Writing

When you are looking to make new friends, think of letter writing. Letters aren't only useful for fixing friendship struggles or making amends when things go wrong, they are also wonderful ways to make new friends. If you are somewhat shy, or nervous about trying to connect with a new friend in person or over the phone, think about writing instead.

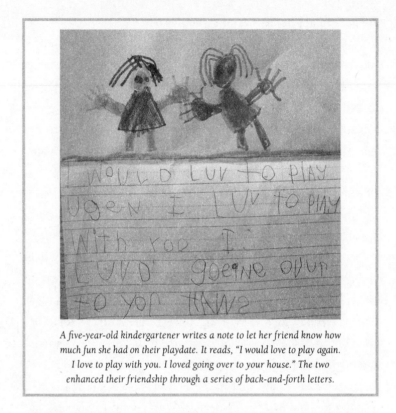

*A five-year-old kindergartener writes a note to let her friend know how
much fun she had on their playdate. It reads, "I would love to play again.
I love to play with you. I loved going over to your house." The two
enhanced their friendship through a series of back-and-forth letters.*

grow and change in the coming months. Therefore, try not to
push too hard (or feel too disappointed) if your child is only able
to imagine a few possibilities as she first contends with the notion
of taking action.

Most important in this step is that *she chooses a solution (or
two or three) that she can live with and feel comfortable about.* While
parents can encourage their daughters to stretch and grow—or
to be challenged in a new way—the crux of the success of this
step is your child's ability to determine her own actions.

Support to act before social struggles occur

As with each of the previous Steps, you can draw on the power and usefulness of this step before social conflict emerges, in areas of her life that have nothing to do with peer relationships. Doing so will allow you both to practice your new approach to problem solving before her emotions are heightened and before she feels the urgency that comes from friendship struggles. Thus, take advantage of the opportunity to support your child to act, allowing her to decide *for herself* the actions she wishes to take, all within the structure and framework of what feels appropriate and possible to you, the supportive parent.

So if you and she have been working together to (for example) problem solve around her organizational issues, now is the time for *her* to decide on a course of action. Will she make a "ready for school" chart to follow? Will she organize her stuff the night before? Or will she choose to take advantage of other options? What she decides is less important than the process you went through together, and that in the end *she* chooses how she will respond to the challenge. Especially with younger children, you will likely be actively involved in helping her successfully follow through on her chosen actions.

When you boil it down, the crux of Step 4, support to act, is to help increase your child's sense of personal power. What this looks like for her right now, and what it looks like six months from now, may be very different. Like anything in life, learning to act effectively takes time and practice, and it involves mistakes. Forgive yourselves! Making room for imperfection will help you and your child to deepen your relationship, and will strengthen her "core."

Observe while supporting to act

In this fourth Step, good observations are essential. That is, you will want to observe how events unfold. When she follows through on her actions, what happens and how does she respond? Of course, your observations may lead to new connections, the need for modified guidance with new decisions about how to further support her to act. Such is the reality of the unfolding dramas that young girls experience.

Role-playing

One powerful tool that you are likely to draw on to help support your daughter to act when confronting sticky situations is *role-playing*. Role-playing is the perfect way to actualize the famous quote by Confucius: "I hear and I forget, I see and I remember, I do

TEACHER'S Tip: Role-Playing

Role-playing is a wonderful way to address social issues in a large group (a single class or a whole grade). For ideas, see "What-If Scenarios," in appendix 2, or use ones relevant to your specific class or situation. Randomly assign students (or hand-select, making sure not to pair up the children who are currently having the identified social issue) to play prescribed roles. Invite onlookers to suggest ways for the participants to respond and amend problematic situations. Feel free to switch students midstream or participate in the role-playing yourself, taking the part of a teacher or a student. This works particularly well to demonstrate a skill you are not sure your students yet grasp. Be sure to point out how different students chose to approach the same problem differently, and how *all* benefited from the support of their peers and classmates in facing tough social issues.

and I understand." While it is possible for your child to listen to or participate in a discussion about what she might say to her friends in a particular situation, being able to *actually do it* is another story. For this reason, engaging in role-playing together will support her to build up a sense of comfort and confidence to face difficult social scenarios.

Before you begin role-playing, you will want to be sure you are both on the same page as far as what the central conflict is, and what goal you are helping your child to achieve. For example, if your child is worried that one of her friends no longer wants to play with her, you might role-play with the goal of your daughter's approaching her playmate and reestablishing a connection. Draw on the dialogue or suggestions the two of you had worked on together while you were guiding her, putting them to use in your role-playing.

Michelle's five-year-old daughter, Maya, faced this issue when Maya began staying for lunch some afternoons at kindergarten enrichment. Maya and Courtney played together most afternoons Maya stayed for lunch, until one day Courtney took the last spot in the Lego center with Reza. Reza and Courtney each stayed every day (as opposed to Maya, who stayed only three days), and the two quickly became best friends, leaving Maya out of the play. Maya was devastated, so she and Michelle worked through the Four Steps. Maya wanted to role-play how she might approach Courtney to reestablish their friendship. Michelle played both a receptive and a rejecting Courtney as Maya rehearsed. By playing each role realistically, you help your child contend with all the possible responses. It took Maya some time (a painful amount of time, in Michelle's opinion) to move from practice to action.

"My mom and me practiced lots of different ways for me to talk to Courtney," reports Maya. "When I was finally ready, I said to Courtney, 'You haven't been playing with me a lot and I've been feeling like you aren't my friend. So, can we make a way to be friends again?' Courtney said, 'Sure I would love to make friends again!' So we made friends again, but we weren't as good friends as we were before. Then we got to be better friends. But it still was not as good friends as we were when we had just met. That's when I knew I had to have more friends. So in the afternoon, I made friends with lots of other kids and I sometimes played with them too."

Not only did role-playing help Maya learn to speak up for herself, she also learned that even when things work out well, they may not be perfect and you may need to make additional decisions as a result (for example, to make some new friends). In this way, role-playing is a way to help your child to turn "good ideas" into "doable actions." One way to increase your child's comfort in taking advantage of role-playing, especially in the beginning, is to give her the option to "press the pause button" at whatever point she needs to along the way. This will encourage her to ask a question, get additional information, check in with you, and so on, and it can help her to feel more confident taking action.

Remind your child (and yourself!) that there is no single right way to approach or resolve a complex problem. Sometimes it takes more than one attempt to find out all the variables that will influence the outcome. Work through as many of these as you might logically think of, but realize that since you cannot control the others involved in the actual interaction, things may not go exactly as planned. All this to say that you are both in this process together, and whatever the outcome, your daughter has you at her side to help her understand, regroup, and reinvest in new strategies as needed.

Integrating the Four Steps

The Four Steps are cyclical and are meant to facilitate your support of your daughter as she works to establish a new set of skills, strengths, and successes. Think of Maya's story—it was only in reestablishing what wound up being a weakened friendship with Courtney that she felt ready to branch out and find new friends (one of the options Michelle had brought up initially when guiding her). In this way, part of your role in utilizing the Four-Step plan is to remain interested but not overly invested in observing how things unfold once your

---

TEACHER'S Tip: Extending Your Caring
Community with Letter Writing

Looking for a way to introduce or extend active Caring Community behaviors? Think letter writing! Ask your students to observe the ways parents or others help them in the classroom. Invite students to form a connection by reaching out with a thank-you note. Choose several children to write letters to a specific helper. As the year progresses, invite all students to write a letter to someone, without needing to have every student write to every helper.

Nine-year-old Sydney Pfeffer writes to Michelle, thanking her for doing "Reader's Theater" with her class. It reads, "Mrs. Anthony, you're the one with the wild smile. You're the one who taught us how to be confident onstage. You're the one who made all of us successful. You're the one who's a miracle worker. You're the one who tells us we'll do great when we're scared to go onstage. So here's a big thank you! You've done so much for us. Thanks! Your actress, Sydney.

daughter takes action (so your daughter knows the actions she chooses are hers to decide), connecting without judgment around what worked and what didn't, and moving forward with additional guidance and support to act, as necessary. The intent is that, through the cyclical process, your daughter is further empowered and the two of you continue to strengthen your relationship.

How Long Will This All Take?

None of these steps (nor the entire process) should take a great deal of time. Sometimes these issues build over time and you only do part of the process at one point, adding other parts as things unfold. In fact, if you spend time observing and connecting with your daughter during peaceful moments—including situations that have nothing to do with social issues—you are likely to find that the time you need to spend on these first two steps during times of crisis is greatly shortened. For example, if you take advantage of the activities in the "Think, Share, Do . . . Activity Bank" at the end of each section, you will likely find that you and your daughter will be in sync and that observation will take but a moment. Establishing this type of relationship in other realms will also allow the connection you have forged to make the transition to guiding feel seamless, quick, and easy. In these instances, the bulk of your energy will be focused on guiding and supporting to act, which may happen at the kitchen table, snuggled up on the couch, or in snitches and snatches as you drive to or from after-school activities.

If you find your child resisting your guidance or seemingly unable to make a decision about a course of action to take, however, consider that you may have rushed too quickly into this phase. If this happens, take a step back and spend some additional time observing and connecting, even if (usually) these Steps are relatively quick.

Be aware that some situations may leave your child feeling vulnerable or emotional. If things get too intense, think about taking a break or distracting her with a change in scene or a new, less intense, joint activity. Facing and dealing with friendship issues may happen quickly, or it may take some time. Please remember that you can never have too many people on your team to support your daughter, so if you need additional help from a teacher, friend, school counselor, or therapist (for her or for yourself), be sure to seek it. When times are good, it is useful to find someone whom you know you can turn to for *your own* guidance. No one gets through life unscathed, so it is good to have a plan for finding additional support in advance. And remember, if you sense your daughter (or another child) is in harm's way, intervene immediately!

3

Think, Share, Do . . .
Activity Bank for Part I

In beginning this journey with your daughter, the goal is to establish rapport and a feeling of safety and comfort. This will let you and your child address social struggles, relational aggression, and girl bullying openly. It is very important that your child not fear being judged ("Why didn't you tell the teacher she did that to you?") or ignored ("I'm sure you'll feel better tomorrow.").

We have organized the Think, Share, Do . . . Activity Banks around the Four Steps, with suggested activities that embody or work toward the main goal of each Step. Sometimes we revisit a single activity in more than one Step; sometimes we highlight an individual Step in a specific activity. Thus, you can approach many, many issues by only attending to a single Step in a given interaction (making a connection with your child one afternoon; supporting her to act on a different day). In this way, the Four Steps can fit into the amount of time you have and can weave around the structure of the interactions you presently engage in with your child. You may choose to do the activities in sequential order as you read, or you can skip around.

Each activity was designed to reach elementary-aged girls at a variety of developmental levels. For younger girls (K–2), you will likely need to provide additional support and explanation, as well as to help them with any reading or writing aspect to the activity. Around third grade, girls become much more independent and will enjoy taking the activities to the "next level." Each suggested activity can be returned to again and again, as your child grows and develops. Whether you are returning to an old favorite or trying out a new experience, invite your daughter to reflect on her own thinking, and encourage her to extend any activity, regardless of her age. Doing so is a wonderful way to observe, connect, guide, and support her to act as she matures.

Introduce the activities by telling your daughter that you have been learning a lot about the ways that girls interact, and that sometimes they don't treat one another very nicely. Let her know that you can imagine how hard it is to try to make or keep friends when sometimes friends are mean, or sometimes they make you feel left out, or sometimes you hear your friends talking about you behind your back, but then other times they are kind to you and want to play. Show her *Little Girls Can Be Mean* and tell her that you are reading a book that has a new way of talking about these problems and has all kinds of ideas and strategies that you can do *together* to problem solve and learn some tips that will make tough situations easier.

STEP 1: OBSERVE

See with new eyes

Remember, in these early days of developing a new framework, you will want to spend some time getting to know your child in a different way. So, observe by *listening* to who your child mentions playing with, *noticing* if her mood changes depending on *who* she played with, or *what activities* they did together, and *thinking about* what her behaviors are like on "good days" versus "bad days." You will then be better at spotting behavior changes as you use the Four Steps.

Tips for Girls: Follow Your Bliss

Each of us has interests or things that we love. If you know yours, see if your parents will help you explore them. You can read about them, join a team or before-school club, sign up for an after-school activity, or ask your parents to teach a skill to you. Be it learning to play cat's cradle, the piano, soccer, or chess, explore what interests you. Not only will it make you happy, it may help you find friends with similar interests as well! Don't worry if it seems unusual. Reyna's daughter, Natasha, has been fascinated with Irish dancing since she was four years old. At six, her parents signed her up for a class. At almost eleven, she is still loving it!

Let the games begin: Start where you are

The more information you have about your child and how she functions as a social being in the world, the more you can build off the skill set she possesses. One valuable piece of information is how she responds to social frustration. To discover this in a safe and nurturing environment, play games!

Playing games as a family is an excellent way to practice a great many necessary social skills, especially the right attitude to winning and losing. For this reason, it is important not to always "let" your child win—that is not what will happen when she plays with her friends. You can gather valuable information about your child's social skills by playing games with her, allowing her to experience and react to both winning and losing.

What does she do when her turn gets skipped time and again in Uno? What does she say (and how does she say it) when her little sister tries to break the rule and go *up* the long slide in Chutes and Ladders? Take stock of her reactions, words, and overall affect. But, remember, now is not the time to comment or guide, just observe, and gather data.

Michelle learned a great deal about five-year-old Maya's developing sense of empathy while playing The Allowance Game with her and eight-year-old Kylie. When two-year-old Bryce came over, insisting they give him coins to put in his pocket, Maya had a strong reaction. But, by resisting the urge to step in and help Maya learn to "share" and "take turns," Michelle observed that Maya actually had no problem handing over a fistful of plastic money, as long as Bryce added the word "please" to his demand. In this way, Michelle was able to see exactly where Maya was in terms of learning social graces, and following rules.

STEP 2: CONNECT

Let the games begin: become her ally

Once you notice the skills your child has, or those she lacks, you can begin to connect with her, using Active Listening or Sharing Stories. Comment without judgment. For example, if you observe that your child is not yet able to be a good sport about winning or losing, you can still connect in a positive way. The goal is to become a team, where she knows you understand her feelings. So in a case like this, think about saying things like:

- ✿ "Huh. I notice that winning is really important to you. What does it feel like when you win? What about when you lose?"
- ✿ "Wow. I can tell from your face that you are disappointed. It's hard to lose sometimes, isn't it? How are you feeling right now?"
- ✿ "Gosh, I remember when I was your age, I just needed to win so badly. When my brother would swoop in and win the game again—ugh!—that made me so mad! Do you ever feel that way when you play Dad and he wins?"

Participate in her world

An important part of connecting with your child is to see the world from her perspective. To help facilitate this, ask your child what *she* wants to do, instead of making your own suggestion. Does she want you to watch one of her favorite shows with her? If so, notice what she finds funny or sad. Engage her in a dialogue where the goal is not to lead her to any new understanding but simply to participate in her world for a few moments. What about reading one of her favorite books together? Or, take her to the park and instead of *watching* her play, join in. Don't teach her a new skill, just revel in her current abilities. Ask her what part you can play in her imaginative scenarios. Build a fort with her and be a member of her royal court. Go on a bike ride and let *her* lead the way. Kick around a soccer ball. Let her steal the ball and score a goal.

One thing Reyna's five-year-old daughter, Nadia, loves to do is to look for crawling critters. Although Reyna is not an insect fan, she delights in studying a fluttering moth, or in laughing together as a ladybug tickles her finger. These moments of connection lead to feelings of togetherness that you both can draw on in times of struggle.

Remember, in contrast to the game-playing activity mentioned above, where you were looking to learn how your child handled challenging situations, your goal here is to laugh, love, and, in this way, connect with and learn from your daughter. Take ten to twenty minutes and get silly with her. Not only will it lighten your worry load for your own life, but it will also help you create shared happy memories—the building blocks of a strong relationship.

Telling tales

Books, videos, and other media are wonderful ways to connect with your child and learn more about her and how she thinks. For example, to approach the topic of empathy, take a *sharing story*

look at *Sam and the Lucky Money* (by Karen Chinn), which is a wonderful tale about a boy who learns to share his Chinese New Year's lucky money. As you read, notice Sam's reaction to the shoeless man and open the door to your child's reaction by asking things like, "How would you feel if you were in that situation?" or "What do you think Sam wants to get with his Lucky Money? What would you like to buy?" At the end of the story, see what your child thinks of Sam's choice, and how her choice may or may not have been the same. Obviously, there are many such books, on various topics.

Don't forget the power of connecting over your child's current interests, by asking questions to see how she has interpreted events in her life. Michelle's eight-year-old daughter, Kylie, loves the musical *Seussical*. It provides the perfect forum to approach numerous social topics. For example, Michelle and Kylie have

---

Tips for Girls: TV Time

Watch one of your favorite TV shows with your mom or dad. Start a conversation about what you notice about how the characters treat each other. What good friend things do they do? What not good friend things do they do? How do the characters show their confidence or lack of confidence? Notice how they carry themselves, their tone of voice, and their facial expressions. Talk to your trusted adult about what kinds of things people are communicating by their bodies, their actions, their reactions, and so on. See if you can turn off the volume and still know how a person is feeling, just by how she carries herself.

connected over what Kylie noticed about Gertrude McFuzz's choices in trying to get Horton the Elephant to notice her, and the powerless position this leaves her in when he is captured by the hunters. Kylie has also talked about Mayzie La Bird and how she makes Gertrude feel when she calls Gertrude plain and brags about her own colorful tail.

These interactions lead to wonderful moments in and of themselves, but using familiar books, videos, CDs, or stories is also a powerful starting point to guide your child to think about *her* choices as she works to make and keep friends.

Admiring her skills

Over the next week, make an effort to observe and connect by acknowledging and admiring some of your daughter's skills.

* *Comment* the next time she gets her laces in a double knot by herself, *remark* that you noticed she is now able to do a handstand or read the directions on her worksheet by herself, *congratulate* her for getting up to fifty jumps without getting tangled in her jump rope.
* Ask her at various points over the next week if she has any small (or large) celebrations she wants to share with you. In Michelle's home, the children came up with their own version of "hip, hip, hooray"; now, any mini victory (or major victory) earns a family "hip, hip, hippo!" at dinner. The evening meal is now sprinkled with these family cheers for anything from two-year-old Bryce's being a good listener to five-year-old Maya braving the dentist. Make these small celebrations a

family event that knows no age or gender boundaries, and see your child's face light up at her own accomplishments.

TEACHER'S Tip: Minicelebrations

You will find that making time for minicelebrations during a class meeting will help build all children's sense of self-confidence. Don't forget the power girls feel at having their classmates celebrate their accomplishments along with them! When Kylie won first place in the Colorado Council for International Reading Association's Young Writer's Award contest, her teacher not only called a special meeting to announce it to the class, but she also individually told every staff member, the principal, and then, by way of the morning video announcements, the whole school. Despite having sprained her knee and chipped her tooth in a bike riding fiasco that weekend (and being—as she put it—"mortified" by having her award announced), Kylie was on cloud nine for more than a week.

STEP 3: GUIDE

Build confidence

Part of making connections with your child and guiding her is to let her know that you see her (and she should see herself!) as powerful and able. Thus for every *one* struggle you and your child identify, you will want to help her also find *two* successes. It is important that she see herself as capable and competent, especially in the early days of identifying problems that will (initially) feel like they have no solution.

❖ Each of you should (privately) make a list of five things your child is good at, capable of, or that she likes about herself. If she cannot yet think of five things, think of three. Better for her to think of fewer things *on her own* than to be told by you what makes her wonderful.

❖ Remember, accomplishments do not need to be grand. Think of seemingly "smaller" things to be proud of. She may be proud that she was the top 11-12 year old swimmer on her team, but she could also celebrate being able to swim a full twenty-five meters without stopping, or even getting into the pool for her first swim lesson! Or, how about learning to tie her shoes or jump rope, mastering her two-wheeler, braving her first sleepover, kicking a goal (or assisting one) in soccer, having the courage to run for student council even though she did not win, or other small victories?

❖ Compare lists. Engage your child in a conversation about what she does well, what new accomplishments she has achieved, or what makes her special. If it was hard for her to come up with a list of things, talk about why this might be.

❖ Save the lists and redo this activity two weeks from today. Was your daughter able to think of more accomplishments? See if she can expand her list to eight or ten items this go around. This is a helpful activity to come back to time and again and serves as a nice way to check in with what each of you sees as her strengths and talents.

TEACHER'S Tip: Student Gems

Tell your students, "I know I have a room full of gems, but some of you don't seem to think of yourselves in that way, and I want to help all of you realize how wonderful and special you are—each one of you! So take five minutes to make a list of all the ways you are special, unique, and wonderful. I can't wait to read your ideas." Have each student write an accomplishment on jewel-shaped paper. Put them in a class "treasure chest." At various points across a week, draw one jewel from the chest and have the class "celebrate" their classmate's accomplishment.

Tips for Girls: Make a Mantra

A mantra is something you tell yourself when you feel nervous, worried, unsure of yourself, or underconfident. It's something to remind yourself that inside, you have the heart of a lion—and the bravery of one too! Michelle's family has the mantra "Boss it!" Kylie and Maya use it to help themselves be the boss of their fears, instead of letting their fears be the boss of them. For example, before a swim meet, eight-year-old Kylie will write the words "BOSS IT!" right beside the listing of her events. This reminder that she is in charge of how she feels, even when she is nervous, helps her center herself before her races. Doing this in realms *other* than just with friends gives her practice, which makes it easier to use in social situations with peers.

Along similar lines, think about adopting the *"Maybe,* but . . ." mantra to combat negative thoughts. So when you catch yourself thinking, "I stink at bike riding," follow this with, *"Maybe,* but . . . I am practicing to get better." Or if you can't help but worry, "Reading is hard for me," add in, "*Maybe,* <u>but</u> . . . I am much better now that I was before!"

Think of your own short saying that helps you feel powerful and that can pull you out of a worried place (or feel free to use "Boss It!" Or "*Maybe,* <u>but</u> . . .") Asking your parents or other trusted adult to help you come up with a mantra is a great way to connect with, get guidance from, and be supported by loved ones as you feel ready to act. Get some puffy paint, jewels, stickers, or other art supplies and decorate a light rock with your mantra. Carry the rock with you in your backpack or pocket and run your fingers over the lettering to remind yourself of your mantra. If you prefer, use letter beads and other types of charms to make a necklace or a bracelet that you can wear as a private reminder of your inner strength!

Let the games begin: guiding more positive interactions

Let's return again to playing games with your child, this time with the intention of guiding her. Give her feedback on what it means to be a good sport, and offer some direct feedback on how her responses and reactions make you—her game-mate—feel. It is only when you point out cause and effect to your child that she is able to understand the consequences of her behavior beyond the immediacy of the emotion she is experiencing. For example, across different games you might say:

❖ "When you cheer as something bad happens to me, like when my player has to go back to Start, you make me feel really bad. It's hard for me to want to play with you when I know you enjoy the game more if I feel awful."
❖ "Part of being a good sport is being a good winner. A

good winner can be proud of herself and what she did but still help her playmate feel good. You could say, 'Wow! I thought of some good strategies to play my last cards. But you did a great job also—you almost caught me before I said *Uno!*'"

✣ "I know how hard it is, but if you want people to want to play games with you, it's really important to know how to be a good loser. A good loser is someone who, even if she's sad to have lost, finds a way to compliment the winner and move forward. When someone is made to feel bad for winning, they're less likely to want to play with you again, and then you lose double!"

✣ "Let's make a list of what kinds of things a good loser

TEACHER'S Tip: Appreciating Community Members

Being a good winner/loser is similar to being a good community member. When you are establishing the guidelines for your Caring Community, dedicate one bulletin board and invite students to tangibly share their appreciation for their classmates! For back-to-school night, post a tree and ask children to write appreciations for the classmates on paper leaves. Direct parents' attention to the board as a way of introducing them to your class guidelines about caring. Be sure each child in your class is appreciated at least once on the board. Change the board to match your units of study and to encourage new appreciations throughout the year. Or, use the board to have classmates celebrate each child when she is Star of the Week or around his or her birthday.

does. Every person in life has to get good at losing, some of the time. *Everyone*. It will really help us to know some specific ways to be a good loser, so the people we care about will want to play with us again. Can you help me think of a list?" Let your daughter take the lead in making a list of ways to become a better winner or loser. For specifics, see "Let the games begin: trying it on for size" in the support to act section on page 72.

Develop cooperative play skills

As your daughter becomes school age, you will likely revel in her ability to engage in projects without you needing to always be there to supervise and direct. As two work-from-home mommies know best, this child-engaged time to get other things done is invaluable. However, when things are quiet enough, independent activities (such as art projects) are also an excellent time to guide your child within cooperative play.

- ✤ Model for your child how you ask for a marker or pen that she is using, or that is out of your reach. Place a marker you know she needs just out of her reach on your side of the table. Help her ask you for it in a way that matches how you would want her to ask her friends.

- ✤ Demonstrate how to make positive, *descriptive* comments on her work, as you continue on yours. See if she will follow suit. Eight-year-old Kylie has heard these kinds of comments so many times, she will often independently announce to two-year-old Bryce, "Wow,

Bryce! You really did an amazing job on your project! I can see how many different colors you used! Hippos for you!" Reyna laughed out loud when five-year-old Nadia complimented, "Mom! The quilt square you're making is so cool. I love the design of the big and small hands together. It's like your hand and Carson's!"

❖ Show your child how to navigate a shared project as you discuss and come to a joint decision about a picture you will draw, and then work together to complete it. Work as a team to make decisions about what materials to use, which colors to include, and who colors each part.

❖ Come up with ideas for a handful of ways you can share your project and develop empathy at the same time. Brainstorm together—maybe you can send it to an out-of-touch relative. Or to a sick friend. Or to your child's teacher, a new neighbor, or even a sick pet. Remember, at this stage in the process, you are simply working together to come up with any and all possibilities; when you support your daughter to act, *she* will actually decide what to do with the project.

STEP 4: SUPPORT TO ACT

Act out of empathy

One way to support your child's ability to navigate social situations is to build up her developing sense of empathy for others. But don't feel you need to be caught in the throes of social strife to approach these topics! As you work on your joint project (see "Develop cooperative play skills," above), the goal is to have a back-and-forth interaction as opposed to just going with your child's suggestion. Support her as she has to modify some of her ideas to find a middle ground. Use this as an opportunity to enhance her negotiation skills, as well as to foster her ability to stand up for ideas or suggestions that matter to her.

Think about choosing another caring project to invest in. During the guiding process, you will have created a list of possibilities (making sure she whittled the list down to ones she would be able/willing to do). Your focus here will be how to support your child as *she* chooses which she would like to act on.

- ✧ Collect change in a large jar. Allow your child to lead the family decision of how to donate the savings. Together you can research different organizations and talk as a family about how you want to support some of the good work going on in your community. If the donation is local, think about having your child hand-deliver the donation. Both of Michelle's girls remember excitedly the day they brought the Giving Jar money—and many dog bones and cat treats—to the Dumb Friends League. We extended the experience by taking the dogs on a walk and hand-delivering them their special treat as well!

- ✧ Visit a neighbor who needs help with (manageable) household chores.

- ✧ Have your child lead the family in gathering together gently used clothing, toys, or books to share at a homeless shelter, home for abused families, or other organization. As part of a social action project in religious school, Reyna's family gathered outgrown shoes to give to needy children. Natasha and Nadia came in from the garage carrying a pair of sparkly snow boots they'd both worn as preschoolers—boots that still made Reyna smile when she looked at them. Natasha announced that they just *had to* give these boots to other kids to enjoy—they were just too amazing to be left collecting dust on the shelf.

❖ Support your child to call a local food bank to see what they need. She can go through your pantry, or create a grocery list and help shop for the food. If your child gets allowance, suggest that she use some of her own money to buy an item or two and see what she says!

Tips for Girls: Friendship Notes

There are lots of ways for you to reach out in caring ways. Doing so creatively can actually help you deepen a friendship.

- Collect art supplies, then ask your parents for special time to write cards or create seasonal decorations for a local children's hospital, veterans' hospital, or other facility. See if your mom or dad will let *you* be the "family representative" to deliver them.
- If it is close to the holiday season, pick out small gifts (such as those from the dollar bins at the store) to wrap and donate to a local charity or less advantaged elementary school. If your parents agree, include a "pen pal" note with the gift, and try to spark a new friendship!

Nine-year-old Emma writes a card for a classmate who was in the hospital. It reads, "Dear X, You are a very great friend. You inspire me every day with your laughter and imagination. Get well soon. Love, Emma." She brought the card over with a teddy bear, and her classmate was so touched, it sparked a new level of friendship between the girls.

Tip for Girls: Take a Stand for Strangers

What better way to practice being assertive than to take a stand on an issue that is important to you? So find out more about a cause that is important to you, talk with your parents about it, and together act on your beliefs. Maybe it will be volunteering at a soup kitchen, writing a letter to your member of Congress about what matters to you, or signing up to support a wildlife conservation fund. Don't let your age stop you. If it matters to you, you can do it! When Michelle's daughter Kylie was four years old, she made colorful bookmarks and sold them to family members over the Internet to raise money for families hurt by the devastating tsunami in eastern Asia. They forwarded her e-mail to their friends, and before she knew it, her e-mail had been sent internationally and Kylie had raised over $450 to donate to the relief efforts!

Let the games begin: trying it on for size

Once your child feels ready to try being a good winner/good loser (see "Let the games begin: start where you are," on page 56), think about supporting her to act on some of the ideas you brainstormed while guiding her. For example:

⋄ *List making*: Encourage your daughter to come up with as many ways to be a good sport as she can (for example, patting the other player's shoulder when she wins and saying, "Good job!"), and add some suggestions along the way. Consider how tone of voice, facial expressions, body language, words, as well as physical proximity convey positive and negative information. As your daughter becomes more aware of how these elements contribute to communication, she will also be more able to recognize and read these social cues.

⋄ *Role-playing*: Set up a dummy situation where the emotional stakes are very low. Pretend you have just won a game and coach your daughter through how to manage the disappointment. Remember to draw on the "good sport" list you have made. Be sure to give her positive

feedback as you do this. You might say, "Than'
smiling when I won. That let me know you might have
been sad, but you were also happy for me." Or, "When
you told me I did a good job when I won, it made me
feel good inside. It made me want to play games with
you again because you were such a good sport."

✿ *"Dry runs"*: With informed participants as players, be
your daughter's coach as she and her older sibling/
father/grandparent play a real game. Support her as she
attempts to apply the new skills she is learning. Give her
permission to "hit the pause button" and refer to her list,
or to ask you a question about how to respond or how
her actions may be perceived by others. Invite the participants to offer (constructive) feedback as well!

Michelle remembers the struggle Maya had in learning how
to be a good sport when playing games with her kindergarten
friends. However, with support to actualize the Four Steps, Maya
realized that friends asked her to play more and she had more
fun (and more opportunities to win) when she said things like,
"I won that time, but let's play again, because maybe this time
you will," or, "It's so much fun to play with you, even if I sometimes lose. Let's play again!" At first these statements sounded
forced. However, with enough practice, Maya not only became
more comfortable saying these things, she actually started to mean
them! Take this opportunity to not only help your daughter develop social skills but also to foster empathy and her ability to
read social cues.

II

The Heart of the Matter:

Applying the Four Steps to

Real Situations Faced by Real Girls

4

Side by Side:
Best Friends, Worst Enemies

It's the day that every parent knows is coming but still dreads: the day when a simple kiss of an elbow or loving hug will not alleviate the pain or fix the problem. Suddenly—before you know it—that day arrives. Your daughter comes home crying and tells you she had a fight with a friend, or your student tells you that she heard the other girls talking about her behind her back (or right in front of her). Hardly out of preschool, she is facing issues that remind you of those you faced in *adolescence;* you cringe. Not sure exactly what to do, and knowing that there is no quick or easy fix, you find yourself staring into your daughter's tear-filled eyes, dumbfounded. Given how young she is, what is she able to understand; what should you say?

Certainly, your own daughter's circumstances and struggles are as unique as she is. Within these pages we will show you how to use the Four-Step process as a road map to navigate your way through the various mishaps your daughter may face.* We will build off the skills your child possesses, to allow the framework and suggestions to further empower her with friends and classmates. In each scenario, we walk you through the Four Steps: observe, connect, guide, and support to act.

We begin by examining "best friend" relationships. Often a girl's entire mood or sense of place in the world is influenced (for good and for bad) by the way she feels about her closest friendships. The gift of these close friendships is that they provide tremendous support to your child. The liability is that girls are often cruelest (intentionally and accidentally) to their best friends. To your child, best friend issues are serious. As we work through the Four Steps, you will see that, while we don't recommend you get mired in that worried place with her, we do recommend you treat her best friend concerns as legitimate. Because, in her world, they are.

Dealing with a Turf War

This story highlights the struggles children go through when a "simple" friendship fight turns into a turf war between best friends. The suggestions apply to scenarios where there is a split between best friends that results in one child's feeling socially isolated and excluded from the larger social scene.

---

*Each story tells a specific tale, but it was chosen for its general theme, which is commonly experienced by girls this age. Each identifies universal strategies regardless of how individual situations may differ.

The In Cursive Club

Michelle walked downstairs one Sunday and found eight-year-old Kylie showing five-year-old Maya how to write her name in cursive. Michelle sat down on the couch beside them. "Maya needed some help with a problem between her and Rachel," explained Kylie. Maya gushed, "It all happened last week when Kylie had her surgery and you weren't home for two whole days. Rachel and me weren't best friends anymore. We weren't any kind of friends. See, Rachel said she knew how to draw cursive. It's true she can draw her name fancy, but it's not cursive. I told her that and she called me a liar, which I am not! So Rachel started an In Cursive Club at recess and made herself the kid-teacher. But she said to me, 'Maya, your name is too hard for you to do in cursive, so you need to get outta here!' I felt really sad 'cause Rachel was no longer my friend and 'cause I couldn't be in the In Cursive Club.

"I knew I had to stand up for myself, so I said, 'Rachel, that is *not* okay that you don't let me in the club!' She glared at me and said, 'Well, I have a great club without you and I'm going to get *everyone* in our class to be in my club *but you*!!' So she offered to teach *all* the kids how to draw their name in cursive except me. I felt really sad. Only Sarah didn't want to be in the club, so we played together. And I had much more fun because all they were doing was digging their name with their finger in the dirt. But I still felt really bad because Rachel stole all the friends and let them be in the club but not me.

"It was like this for a lot of days and I felt really sad without anyone to play with at recess. But then Lucy said, 'This club is too boring. All we do is draw in the dirt. I don't want to come here anymore.' Rachel said, 'Please please stay, it's the best club you will ever see. It will be so much fun. You'll write in cursive stories.' That's when Lucy said, 'I don't know how to write in cursive and you're not teaching very well. Besides, they are the ones having fun at recess.' So she came to play with me and Sarah. And then all the other kids went off too—they went off to play and left the In Cursive Club behind, which made Rachel mad, but also kinda sad, so she didn't do the In Cursive Club on Friday. I do want to learn cursive, so if I *want* to be in the In Cursive Club I can, but I don't have to. That is why I asked Kylie to help me."

What happened and why?

As commonly happens in young girls' friendships, a major fight is often instigated by a minor issue. Here, Maya's offhand remark that Rachel didn't know cursive, even though she claimed she did, was a big deal. For Rachel, this was publicly humiliating and proof that Maya was not being a friend (Maya was calling her unskilled or a liar). And as we often see with children this age, Rachel formed a club—in this case, the In Cursive Club. Leveraging how fun the club would be, Rachel used the friendship break to socially isolate Maya by inviting "all the other kids" and excluding Maya. Thus, as is common, the situation escalated beyond a one-on-one friendship issue between two girls. The escalation *included* but didn't *involve* the other children. Meaning, the other children were not ganging up on Maya to be mean, they were just pawns in the dynamic between Rachel and Maya. Rachel showed her immensely powerful reach (to "everyone in the class"), but the other children were only peripherally involved.

This is a common result of a "best friend" friendship gone awry: a small problem that quickly gets bigger to the point that other kids are caught in the mix. The developmental level of the kindergarteners kept this situation relatively tame. If the girls had been fourth graders, Rachel would most likely have been more active in getting the kids to take *sides,* as opposed to just trying to entice the kids to join the club. It is unclear if literally *all* the children were involved, or if it just *felt* this way to Maya, which is something we explore further in our examination of how Maya and Michelle worked through the Four Steps.

What Maya did well

She stood up for herself: When the fight ensued, Maya made no bones about telling Rachel that excluding her from the club was not okay. Unfortunately (but not surprisingly), Rachel's response was to dig her heels in and expand the exclusion: Not only was she going to have a club, but it was going to be with everyone in the class *except* for Maya. As disappointing as that was, the more important skill shone through: When our friends treat us badly, we need to stand up for ourselves. Sometimes the outcome is good, sometimes it is not, but either way, we are worthy of respect!

She allowed herself to connect with another child: Once an exclusion happens, the offended child often feels so hurt that connecting with another child is not possible, at least not initially. Sarah approached Maya, and Maya managed to be open to the connection. Sarah has a great heart, and we as parents want to be on the lookout for the Sarahs of the world—they are girls whose friendship with our children we want to encourage! Maya felt enough "in the right" to be able to connect with Sarah, despite also feeling ostracized and excluded "by the whole class."

She found additional support: Not only did Maya find a connection with another friend, she also found a resource to teach her the skill she felt she needed to allow her to join the club (asking her sister to show her how to write her name in cursive). When girls are well versed in the Four Steps, they are often able to actualize them on their own, even at a very young age!

She actively connected with her mom around a social issue, even if after the fact: Not only had Michelle been away from home when this incident occurred, but the family attention was on Kylie's surgery and recovery. Thus, Maya had to face this social issue alone, with Michelle only finding out after the fact. While there is no worse feeling than not being there in your child's hour of need, it happens. But when that happens (and it will), you can still take advantage of the Four Steps.

Applying the Four Steps: Strategies to use with your own daughter

STEP 1: OBSERVE

"Come back" after a time away: Mom was not able to observe the social situation as it unfolded, or to notice her daughter's at-home reaction to it. However, there was still an opportunity to observe here. Michelle walked in and saw her daughters drawing together. You can imagine being the parent thinking, "Yes! The girls are happily engaged. Now is my chance to get some things done." However, you can learn a lot from just watching your children interact. Sitting next to your child is also a silent but powerful way to both observe and connect. One surefire way to bond with your daughter and to invite open discussion is to establish proximity or display physical affection. When Michelle sat down beside her girls, instead of continuing to play or showing Michelle their creations, they initiated a conversation about a topic of importance.

Forgive your absences: The other thing to observe here is that Maya's story happened while Michelle was away and unaware. Forgive yourself for not always being there, and know that *not* being there provides opportunities for your child to grow and show you what she is capable of on her own. When you can, try to take some time to ask your child how things have been going, to kick a ball with her or play a board game, or comment on how you have been really busy and miss having time to talk with her

---

TEACHER'S Tip: Observing for Clubs

Clubs and group social exclusions often take place on the playground, away from teachers' supervising eyes. So take a few moments to observe your students before and after lunch or recess. Are there children who seem more apprehensive or withdrawn than usual? This may be your cue to take advantage of the Four Steps!

each day. Doing so will let your child know how much she means to you, and it will open the door for her to share things that you have missed.

STEP 2: CONNECT

Employ Active Listening, including empathy: Draw on Active Listening to help your child tell her story or to comment on the information she shares with you. Here Michelle was able to say: "Maya, I am really amazed at how brave you were. It is really hard to be able to stand up for yourself, especially when you are feeling sad and left out. How did it feel to tell Rachel that she was not allowed to exclude you from the club?" Michelle was also able to draw on empathy and say, "Maya, I can imagine it would be really hard to lose your best friend and not have your mom or sister around to talk to. What did you do to help yourself through such a tough situation?" If you can help your child see herself as

---

TEACHER'S Tip: Lunch-Bunch "Club"

If you notice certain girls always on the outside of friendship circles or clubs, why not invite them to join yours? At this age, teachers are adored by their female students. So take this opportunity to connect with your ousted, lonely, or isolated students and invite a few to have a weeklong lunch-bunch "club" with you. Think about having each invite a classmate along. It may be just what the doctor ordered to boost their confidence, or increase their social "value" in the eyes of their peers.

brave and resourceful, you can better guide her and help her build on the skills she possesses.

STEP 3: GUIDE

Obviously, the urgency of the issue had passed by the time Michelle was made aware of it, but the learning opportunities it provided remained. In fact, children's retroactive discoveries are often the most productive ones because they are not made in panic mode.

Identify the instigating factor: Here, while it seemed to Maya that Rachel turned on her out of the blue, there is another perspective: Maya having told Rachel that she couldn't write in cursive may have accidentally started the argument. Of course, your goal is not to make your own child feel bad, but rather to help her reflect back on a situation that could have been handled differently, with a possibly different outcome.

TEACHER'S Tip: Hot Potato

Sometimes girls make rash decisions when they are mad. Hot potato is a fun activity to get kids talking about what it feels like to be mad, and how to manage it. Talk to your students about how anger is a "hot" feeling—it makes you feel hot inside, or on your face. Tell them, "When you end up with the hot potato, I want you to imagine feeling mad. Think about what makes you feel that way. Share with the group a positive way to deal with that feeling." Come back to this game at various points in the year and hear how the children's strategies have expanded!

Survey her friendship circle: Nothing feels better than having a best friend. Best friends are those we can count on in a pinch, who make us laugh, and who share in our joys and sorrows. However, because of the intensity and exclusivity of a best friend relationship, best friends are also a tremendous social liability. So often, girls have one favored friend they share with and continuously seek out. In doing so, they become dependent on this one person to fill a great many needs. What if she is absent one day? What if she wants to make new friends? What if the two get in a fight? As wonderful as best friends are, we are strong advocates of supporting children in having *more than one* close friend, or at least in maintaining multiple friendships alongside a "best friendship."

Maya's situation is a case in point. Because Maya invested all of her "friend time" in Rachel, she was less available to *also* be friends with other girls. When Rachel turned on her, Maya felt

---

TEACHER'S Tip: Supporting an Ousted Student

How can you support an "ousted" student? Ask her what she can do to keep herself safe, even if the bully (Mean Girl, ex-friend) never changes her behavior. The goal here is to help your students realize that they can't think that they will only be safe when there are no bullies, or friend fights, or Mean Girls—because there always will be! Instead, they need to understand that they will be safe when *they are no longer a potential victim for a bully*, when they find social alternatives outside of the present conflict. See "Help her identify her allies," below, for ideas on how to do this.

completely alone. This was magnified by Rachel asserting her social power, literally saying she would get everyone in the class to be in her club but Maya. This was a good time to talk with Maya about the limitations of a best friend, and to work together to think of other girls she might like to become better friends with, to expand her social options.

Help her identify her allies: One role of loving parents is to help make situations that feel overwhelming to our children more "tackle-able." Here Maya talked about how "all of the kids" in her class were in the In Cursive Club. This perception left her feeling vulnerable, alone, and powerless. Even though none of those other children was actively trying to hurt Maya, she felt and responded as if they all were!

Unfortunately, it is all too common that a best friend problem can suddenly include other children, but the others are often bystanders to the conflict between the two girls. Thus, while it is no doubt true that the friendship break with Rachel left Maya feeling like she was alone, the reality was that Maya could have reached out to other classmates to buoy herself up, if she had realized she was *not* isolated from everyone and if she felt capable of doing so. Maybe it is true that *every* child in the class did this or did that, but that does not mean that every child is *purposefully against* your child, or even aware of the fight, and girls need to see the difference . . . who are your child's other allies, and how can she reach them?

Tips for Girls: Assert Yourself!

Learning how to interact with peers while being kind and respectful can be hard, especially as you try to reach out to new friends. Some girls are at one end of the spectrum now—they are often too nice (so they get taken advantage of). Others are at the other end—too controlling (so they take advantage of too many others). Most are somewhere in between the two. A perfect balance of niceness and control is to strive to be *assertive*.

Being *assertive*—balancing niceness and control—is a way of carrying yourself and interacting with others. It says, "I care about myself. I know my ideas are important. I deserve to be treated with respect!"

Choose three items from the list below and practice them in front of the mirror. Try saying the same comment in three ways, changing the meaning by the way you say it and/or by changing your facial expression or body language. Sentences like "She's so cool," "Nice dress," or "I can tell you studied really hard for that test" can mean very different things, depending on *how* you say them! Try to say each sentence first so that you sound and seem *passive*, then try a more *aggressive* tone and body posture. Finally, end saying each sentence *assertively.* When you end being assertive, the feeling in your body and your tone of voice will stay with you longer! *Acting* confident (even if you are not quite sure of yourself) will help people *see* you as confident, *treat* you as confident, and help you then *feel* confident inside yourself!

An assertive, confident person:
- Keeps her shoulders back
- Holds her head high
- Looks other people right in the eye/face

- Speaks with "I messages" (see page 91 for more)
- Uses confident body language
- Speaks in a strong but kind/friendly tone of voice
- Uses relaxed, friendly facial expressions
- Stands close to another, but not in her personal space, to show connection

TEACHER'S Tip: Identifying Potential Friends

If you notice a child is being ostracized or seems socially isolated, encourage her to be a detective. Ask her, "Who are the kids who get along with everyone?" "Who are the ones who say positive things to others?" "Who shares easily?" Then, encourage your student to reach out to or seek to be included by the children *she has identified* as friendly and kind.

STEP 4: SUPPORT TO ACT

Strengthen new friendships: There are many benefits to having a cluster of friends (over one exclusive best friend). With the sting of this exclusion still resonating in Maya's head, it was the perfect time to encourage her to branch out and make new friends. Michelle took the opportunity to point out to Maya that when someone like Sarah goes against the grain and stands by her, this friend is someone to appreciate. If you find your daughter in a similar situation, think of other friends for your child to connect with.

> **TEACHER'S Tip:** Responding to Clubs
>
> When clubs or cliques get in the way of your Caring Community, you have a role to play in helping children realize what is happening and guiding them to change. You can address the class and say, "I notice there is a club going on that is interfering with my ability to teach and your ability to learn, and it has gone against what we are working towards in our Caring Community. What can we do about this? [Take suggestions.] Knowing that members of our class are being excluded hurts all of us, so if you are approached by children to be in a club that excludes others like this, be strong and refuse to be part of something that goes against our class goals." Or talk to particular children seperately. You will be amazed at the influence you have!

Repair old friendships: After fights such as these resolve in one way or another, your child can decide if it is time to move on from the friendship, or to try and repair what was broken. Both choices provide opportunities to admire different qualities (for example, a child's ability to risk taking a break from her best friend versus her ability to forgive her friend and fix the friendship).

While you may be wary about trusting a child like Rachel again, it is more important that *your child* be the one making the decisions about how to run her own social life. Just be sure that in her excitement to re-friend her "Rachel," she does not exclude or forget the kindness shown by her "Sarah." Meanwhile, you can again observe, connect, guide and support to act as her choices unfold.

Tips for Girls: Developing "I Statements"

"I statements" are a great way to move from being *passive* (like a doormat) or *aggressive* (like a Mean Girl) to being *assertive* (kind, but standing up for yourself). They are usually done in a very specific way, and they can be used anywhere, at any time, with anyone.

1. "I feel _____ (mad, sad, disappointed, jealous, upset, scared, worried, nervous and so on)
2. when you _____ (describe the action or behavior),
3. because _____ (say how this action led to your feeling).
4. I need you to/I want you to/I wish you would _____ (say what you would like the other person to do).

Here's an example from Michelle's family:

When five-year-old Maya slid down the couch pillows to land on eight-year-old Kylie, who was reading on the floor, Kylie shrieked, "Maaaayaaaa! Stop it! You ran into me!" Maya got defensive and said, "Well, you were in the way!" Nothing was accomplished. Why?

These types of "you" statements (statements that tell others what they are doing wrong or what they need to do) can seem bossy, or even like you are being aggressive or like a Mean Girl. Better to solve the problem with an "I statement!" The next time it happened, Kylie tried: "Maya, I feel squinched when you slide on top of me because I was here first. I wish you would move your pillow slide to the other side of the couch." Less defensive, Maya happily adjusted her pillows and Kylie felt better that her "emergency" was resolved. All with a simple "I statement!"

Here's an example from Reyna's family:

In the car, ten-year-old Natasha was singing along to a CD. Five-year-old Nadia screamed, "Stop singing so loud! Stop, stop, stop!" Natasha got angry and said, "The rule is I can sing as long as I'm singing the real words. I'm NOT stopping!" Nadia kept screaming and so Natasha just sang louder.

Reyna pulled over and reminded Nadia about "I statements." Nadia tried, "Natasha, I feel sad when you sing so loud because then I can't hear the music. I need you to sing softer so that we can both have fun with the song." Natasha didn't feel like she'd been yelled at anymore and was much happier to use a softer voice.

Remember: Part of getting good at "I statements" is also getting good at listening to how *others* feel. How to be a good listener is one thing assertive girls learn that aggressive girls do not. The biggest difference between a bully and a leader? Her ability to listen!

Now you try it! Read the below "you" statements (notice that some may *seem* like "I Statements" but are really "you" statements). In your journal, turn them into "I statements:" "I feel ___ when you ____ because ____. I wish you would____."

You Statements:

"Lacey, stop pulling my hair!"

"Trevor, you have taken over the whole reading area. I need room for my project too! Move over!"

"You promised to do the science project with me, but now you are partnered with Terren. How could you break your promise like that?!"

"I think this is a free country so I can do what I want and you can't tell me what to do. You need to let me join the game."

When Best Friends Pull Away

This story highlights the struggles children go
through when a best friend moves away from the
intensity of the friendship. The suggestions apply to
scenarios where one best friend pulls away
from the other, sometimes in hurtful ways,
often for unknown reasons.

Ellie Dumps Hailey

"It seemed like such a simple issue," Hailey's mother recalls. "I have no idea how it turned into such a complicated mess!" Mom goes on to share how Hailey and Ellie (now in first grade) had been best friends since preschool. In January, Ellie and Hailey decided to audition for the talent show together: One girl was going to stand on her head while the other held her ankles.

However, days before the audition, Ellie told Hailey she didn't want to be in the show. Hailey came home that day saying that Ellie was "being mean." Mom told Hailey that things would probably work out the next day. When they didn't, Hailey began to follow Ellie around, asking Ellie if she was mad at her, if she had done something wrong, and so on. Ellie would not acknowledge Hailey at all. In Hailey's words, "Ellie dumped me." That night, Hailey barely ate her dinner, telling her parents she wasn't hungry. Mom knew something was wrong and told Hailey firmly that she needed to tell her what was going on. She was surprised to hear Hailey's tears were still about the talent show auditions and Ellie being mean. Mom tried to explain to Hailey that sometimes kids get nervous before something like a talent show, and she would need to be understanding.

The next day, Hailey told Ellie that she was okay about her not wanting to do the talent show; that she didn't want Ellie to do something that would make her sad. Suddenly, Ellie shouted that she *did* want to do the show, just not with Hailey. She walked off and began happily playing with Zunera, leaving Hailey heartbroken. Becca came over to Hailey and said, "I'll do the show with you." Hailey reluctantly agreed. Throughout school, Hailey was quiet and disengaged. The teachers were apparently unaware of any issue.

By the time Mom picked Hailey up, Hailey was in tears. Her mother tried to comfort her, saying she was sure that Ellie would be in a better mood tomorrow, that Hailey had many other friends, and that maybe it was time to set up some playdates with some new girls like Becca. Although Hailey agreed, she remained despondent the rest of the night.

What happened and why?

Girls in the early school-age years are just learning how to make and keep sustained friendships. Researchers such as Dr. JoAnn Deak, in her book *Girls Will Be Girls*, report that while certain girls will "click" and become "best friends," most children this age want and need to experience multiple, less intimate friendships. As Maya, Hailey, and countless other girls in elementary school have learned the hard way, having a number of friends within your circle is a protective device, so that losing one friend doesn't mean the loss of all social possibilities. Even in close friendships, it is not unusual to have one friend try to pull away, and to need to do so in a way that causes excruciating pain to the other. And while Ellie may seem unkind, or even mean, her actions are typical and expected (see page 181 for Ellie's version of the story). As Dr. Michael Thompson reports, in *Best Friends, Worst Enemies*, "Some of it *is* cruel. They are trying out their social power, and that includes the power to hurt." The reality is, it is very difficult for a child to invest heavily in more than one deep friendship at a time. Thus, for Ellie to try to make new friends, she has to first pull away from her close relationship with Hailey, at least temporarily.

What Hailey did well

She actively participated in friendship: Despite being only seven years old, Hailey was exceedingly loyal. She was looking to have memorable experiences such as the talent show with her best friend. When things went awry, Hailey tried to figure out why by asking Ellie a series of questions. Despite being heartbroken, she remained open to forming new friendships with other girls, such as Becca.

She sought out help in an age-expected manner: Early on in the conflict, Hailey reached out to her mom in a very "kid" way, telling her how Ellie was "being mean." When parents are better able to hear these comments as children's attempts to initiate discussions about social issues, the door is open to apply the Four Steps, as outlined below.

She remained open to parental influence: Girls this age are extremely receptive to adult influence and guidance. When parents apply the Four Steps, they can have a significant impact on their child's social choices and sense of agency in friendship struggles.

Hailey's mom was not versed in the Four-Step plan. Thus, it took some time for Mom to realize the social struggle Hailey was facing. That notwithstanding, when she told Hailey that she needed to confide in her, Hailey did. Hailey then tried hard to take her mother's advice, telling Ellie that she didn't want her to do something that would have made her sad. She also remained open to her mother's later suggestion to solidify her connection with Becca.

Applying the Four Steps: Strategies to use with your own daughter

STEP 1: OBSERVE

Be on the lookout: Young girls often struggle to understand new and confusing emotions. Why is she being so mean? Did I do something wrong? Whom will I play with at recess? These are questions girls commonly ask themselves but often will not ask their parents, unless *parents* initiate the discussion. Thus, one of your first jobs is to listen to your child in new ways. While you don't want to anxiously interview your child or create problems that aren't there, you do want to observe her and notice changes. Some ways young girls "communicate" that something may be awry:

- Increased fights with siblings
- Increased lethargy or exhaustion
- Increased complaints of illness (headaches, stomachaches)
- Increased complaints about school
- Shorter temper
- Increased or decreased appetite (repeatedly saying she is not hungry, or eating as a coping mechanism)
- Increased crying about unrelated things
- Pretend play that includes more Mean Girl behavior or stories with negative components
- Negative comments about her teacher
- Talk about how so-and-so is "being mean" or is "not my friend anymore"
- Talk about wanting to stay inside for recess, or not go to music class, or asking for a note to miss gym because it is too cold
- Increased "fishing" questions directed at parents or teachers: "When you were little, did your friends ever dump you?"

Remember, your child is an individual and she may show her worries in her own unique way that you have yet to learn.

Michelle's clue that Kylie was stressed about social issues was when she would "overworry" about unrelated events, such as how much pollution there was in the world, or when she began to talk about "hating reading" or not liking theater anymore—her favorite pastimes. If you notice these types of behaviors, or a collection of them, it might be time to connect with your daughter and open a discussion around friendship issues.

STEP 2: CONNECT

After observing something may be amiss (or if your child comes to you directly), we encourage you to make concerted efforts to connect with her in ways she can discern and understand.

Be an Active Listener: Because parents can't directly affect the choices of *other* children (for example, make Ellie do the show with Hailey), they may feel they have little to offer other than a vague, "You'll work it out, I'm sure." The power of Active Listening is that you don't have to—and in many ways, shouldn't—"fix it." You are simply trying to connect with your child, and to listen. When you can let go of needing to find a solution for your child at this point in the process, you actually become more "available" to hear the message behind her words.

Sometimes girls need both a specific invitation to share their experiences and also the room to tell their stories, share their thoughts, or voice their confusions. While it was very useful for Mom to offer Hailey insight into *why* Ellie may have been acting the way she did, it was equally important to Actively Listen to Hailey as she expressed her disappointment or sadness. For example, Mom might have said, "Hailey, you sound disappointed that Ellie doesn't want to do the talent show with you." Or, "It sounds like you're worried that you're losing Ellie as a friend."

Really listening to and helping your daughter put words to her emotions will go a long way to allowing her to identify and articulate the problem, and *let it go*. So often, entire days of learning are lost when girls are wrapped up in social struggles. If you can use the connection part of the Four-Step plan to support your daughter in talking about her feelings, you can help her to get the most out of school while she is there—because she knows there is support waiting for her at home.

See the world from her perspective: How often do you hear your daughter announce that a friend, sibling, or classmate is being mean? While empathizing at each occurrence would mean that nothing in life would get done, letting your child know that you understand her world and sympathize with what she is experiencing *some* of the time will go a long way. Try making a comment like, "Wow, it must be really frustrating to plan your talent show act with Ellie and then have her pull out at the last minute. I can imagine you might feel really mad about it." Helping your daughter talk about what she is *currently* sad about (her disappointment about the talent show) will solidify her trust in you as someone to come to with *future* struggles, as much as it will help her come to terms with her "right now" struggle.

Avoid the quick fix: We all do it, and there is nothing wrong with it some of the time. But it is worthwhile to make a concerted effort to hold yourself back from trying to solve the problem or gloss over it. When Hailey's mom told her that Ellie was probably in a bad mood and would feel better tomorrow, she was trying to make Hailey feel better. Unfortunately, such attempts often backfire, and the girl you care about feels worse because she then feels alone in her dismissed worries. Even if Ellie had been in a better mood the next day (and there is no guarantee she would have been!), that would not have changed the pain and struggle Hailey had been feeling for the days prior. Following the Four-Step plan will let you meet both your desire to help and your child's desire to be heard.

Help your child to open up: Hailey's mom knew something was amiss when Hailey did not eat dinner. Rather than continue to offer vague reassurances or say something like, "I'm here to talk if you need me," Mom told Hailey she knew something was wrong and directed Hailey to tell her about it.

In contrast to adolescence, elementary-aged girls are very responsive to parents being involved in the details of their lives. Girls of this age need specific invitations and even directed guidance to know exactly *how* to open up. To help your own child learn to see you as an ally and respond to your encouragement to share her worries, try out some of the suggested activities in the "Think, Share, Do . . . Activity Bank" at the end of this part.

STEP 3: GUIDE

Once you have observed a problem and connected with your daughter, you can begin to provide guidance. Doing so will encourage her to realize the many options *she* has in a situation, even if she cannot control what *her friend(s)* might do.

Brainstorm a series of possibilities: One of the most active roles for children in the guiding phase is to participate in creating a list of possibilities. So embrace any and all suggestions and whittle down the list to only those she (and you) are willing and able to follow through on *after* her participation has been fully welcomed. Initially, you might find some of your child's suggestions to be unrealistic, such as suggesting changing schools or *forcing* Ellie to do the show. Rather than dismiss her contributions, you can simply list each option, saying, "Yep, that's one idea. What others can you think of?" Of course, you should add your own more realistic suggestions as well.

What elements does she control?: Girls often feel the acute need to solve the problem before they can let it go. Yet your child does not control all aspects of a situation. In addition, she may not be ready (or it may not be wise) to confront certain aspects of the problem immediately. Help your daughter understand that there may be aspects of a situation she needs to "leave be," while *other* aspects can be problem solved and acted upon. If you help your daughter plan her next move based on the elements of the situation she *can* influence, you give her back control. For example, Hailey couldn't make Ellie be kind, like

Michelle's daughter Kylie wrote a letter to her friend after Kylie won the election for class representative. "Dear X, You must be disappointed you didn't win. Truth is, I admire you. My goal is to become as nice as you. Tell you what. How 'bout you tell me your ideas and I'll report them to student council the following council meeting. Thank you for setting an example! Your friend forever, Kylie."

her again, or want to do the talent show with her. Given what had happened previously, it may not have been wise for Hailey to continue to approach Ellie to try to figure out what had gone wrong. However, Hailey could have focused on the elements she *could* control: inviting Becca to do the talent show with her.

STEP 4: SUPPORT TO ACT

After you and your daughter have had a chance to evaluate the situation and brainstorm some new strategies to confront it, it is time to support her in actively solving the problem. Too of-

Dear ████

I'm sorry there can't be two class representitives. You must be disapointed. I know what thats like. I've expierieced the same thing. The truth is, I admire you. My goal is to become as nice as you. Tell you what, How about you tell me any idea's you have about making our school a better place. I'll report that thought to Student Cousil the rollowing meeting. That way, you could be a part of helping our school.

your friend forever,

Kylie

As you can see, while the first letter was very nice, Michelle helped Kylie reword certain parts to better express herself. The guided version reads, "Dear X, I'm sorry there can't be two class representatives. You must be disappointed. I know what that's like. I've experienced the same thing. The truth is, I admire you. My goal is to become as nice as you. Tell you what. How about you tell me any ideas you have about making our school a better place. I'll report that thought to student council the following meeting. That way, you could be part of helping our school. Your friend forever, Kylie."

ten, girls will either bury their emotions or dwell on them, so it is your job to help her actualize her goals.

Write a letter or draw a picture: Even a very young girl can write a basic letter (or dictate one to you), telling her friend how she feels. Remember, she does not have to send it! *One word of caution*: letters, especially e-mails, have permanence to them. You will likely want to read over your child's letter and provide any necessary guidance before she sends it. Read it with a careful eye—if there are things in there your daughter may later regret saying or that she would not want another child to see, it's best either to edit the letter or use this as a private learning and venting experience rather than actually sending it.

Face the problem right away?: Ask your daughter if she wants to try to talk to her friend about how she feels right away, or if she wants to wait and see how the sand settles in a few days. Social problems that can be left alone for a few days often just disappear. If she feels she wants/needs to do something right away, think about role-playing with her to help her learn to share most appropriately how she feels. You might say something like, "Pretend that I'm Ellie, and I'm playing with Zunera. How can you get my attention? You need my attention before you can tell me what you are thinking or feeling. Great. Now that I'm looking at you and listening, what might you say to me about how you feel about not doing the talent show together?"

Help your child carry through on a specific plan of action: When Hailey fell apart after the second day, her mother rightly suggested connecting Hailey with other friends, and named a concrete way to do so (setting up a playdate with Becca). Girls at this age are still concrete thinkers who need structured guidance to actualize ideas. Thus, telling a young child to reach out to new friends is too general; instead, she needs you to help her know *what* that reaching out might look like. She will likewise need support to *follow through* on the steps needed to do it.

❖ Help your daughter choose a friend to call and set up a playdate.

✿ Encourage her to reach out to a new friend. This can be as simple as approaching someone specific in her class and saying, "Hey, do you want to sit together at lunch/ play together at recess?"

✿ Don't forget to encourage friendships with girls in other classes. Having a friendly face on the playground that is not among the ones she needs to learn beside will offer your daughter social options.

TEACHER'S Tip: Supporting Friend-Making

When appropriate, encourage your student to exchange contact information with a specific girl in class whom you think would make a good match socially, academically, or both. Encourage her to show enthusiasm, talking about how much fun it would be to play together after school. Suggest that she set up a specific time that they will try to call one another.

Yo-Yo Friendships

This story highlights the struggles children go through when they are trapped in yo-yo friendships, where their closest friends do very hurtful things but then balance this out with doing very loving and supportive things. The suggestions apply to scenarios where children are caught in an unrelenting hot/cold cycle of a loving-and-abusive friendship.

When friendship is both loving and abusive

Third graders Grace and Ashley had been best friends for over a year. They both loved unicorns, soccer, and putting on plays. They were two of the smartest and most eager kids in the class, so it was no surprise that the teacher often paired them up. One day in May, the class was working on their Reader's Theater plays. Although both girls had wanted to be the unicorn, one had to settle on being the dragon. Wanting to support her best friend, Grace agreed to play the beast. It was Ashley who had brought up the idea of using Sharpie markers to draw scales on Grace's arms—to let their play be really realistic. "Since I get to be the unicorn, let's give you a really cool costume. This will let you look like a real dragon!" Grace thought it had indeed been great fun to outline the red and green scales all up and down her arms.

Until Mrs. Kennedy saw her. She was furious! Grace had never seen her so mad. No amount of scrubbing in the bathroom got the permanent marker off her skin. Grace tried to hide her tears and cover her arms the rest of the day. She dreaded having to show her mother. Stunned at seeing her, her mother asked what Grace had been thinking when she'd drawn on her arms. "I guess I wasn't really thinking," Grace stammered. "Me and Ashley were just having so much fun making me a really cool costume . . ." Her voice trailed off. Mom said, "It seems to me that when you and Ashley are together now, you *often* don't do a lot of thinking. Let me guess. It was *Ashley's* idea to mark up your arms." Feeling defensive, Grace lied, "No! It was my idea. I wanted to look like a real dragon!"

The next day was Field Day and the class T-shirt was short-sleeved. When Grace expressed dismay, her mom said sympathetically, "It's going to be hot today and sometimes we have to live with the choices we make." At school, Ashley went over to Grace and offered to let Grace wear her sweater. She said, "I told my mom about it last night and she got mad too. It was a bad idea and I'm sorry you wrote on yourself in pen." When the girls noticed Hannah snickering, Ashley was quick to stand up for Grace. "That's not nice, Hannah. Why don't you mind your own business? Can't you see she feels bad about it already?" Grace felt glad to have a friend who understood. Someone she could trust to stand up for her.

A few weeks later, Grace was over at Ashley's house. The two were putting on a play. Ashley had given Grace the choice of which part she wanted—the mother or the baby. "The *baby* is the really good part," Ashley told her. "You should get the really good part this time, since I got to be the unicorn." Grace happily agreed—that *was* the best part! Ashley even brought out the Flip® video camera she had gotten for her birthday. They could tape themselves and then watch their performances. They were BFFs and so they promised never to show the video to anyone else.

But in school a few days later, Hannah walked by and said, "Grace, do you need a *diaper change*?" Grace panicked. She had worn a diaper as part of her costume in the play with Ashley, but Ashley had sworn she would never tell anyone or show anyone the video. Later that morning, Hannah said loudly to Mallory, "Look, I'm Grace," as she sucked her thumb. *Ashley would never betray me like that. It was Ashley's idea that I wear the diaper anyway—the good costume to go with the good part,* Grace told herself, but now she wasn't so sure. *How did Hannah find out? Who else did Ashley show the video to?* Suddenly, Grace didn't feel very well—she thought she felt a headache coming on.

What happened and why?

Grace found herself in one of the most destructive and confusing peer situations there is: a *yo-yo friendship.* Like the name entails, yo-yo friendships are those where one girl is systematically embraced and rejected—supported and betrayed—over and over in an ongoing exertion of control by the more powerful friend. Unfortunately for her, the victimized girl is a participant in the ongoing situation, because she is confused. No sooner has her friend done something (that could be construed as) cruel than has she also done something (obviously) loving and kind. Part of the confusion stems from the fact that, because of the level of intimacy between the girls (yo-yo friendships by definition occur in close relationships, usually an individual friendship pair, but they can also be a pairing that is part of a larger group), the cruel acts are often subtle, hidden, or easily explained away.

As you can see in this scenario, one could tell the story from Ashley's perspective without painting her as the villain. Like most other yo-yo situations, if you isolate two or three incidents, you can scarcely make out a systematic pattern. In fact, some of the "incidents" can be reasonably explained or justified. It is only over time, through a collection of such incidents, that you are able to fully identify the pervasive manipulation and control one girl yields over the other. One aspect of yo-yo friendships that makes them unique is how each girl perceives the relationship. That is, in normal friend conflict, both individuals worry about the loss of the friendship. In a yo-yo situation, the bully does not. As you will see in going through the Four Steps, these relationships are often the most difficult to support your child to navigate or to break away from, because the girls themselves are so loyal to their friends. It can take weeks, months—sometimes even *years*—for parents or the girls themselves to realize the destructive toll the friendship is taking on their sense of self-esteem and self-worth.

What Grace did well

She sought a friend who shared her interests and abilities: Grace had chosen a friend with a number of qualities that most parents would say they hope for: intelligence, good manners, interests and talents that overlap with their own child's. Initially, it seemed to be a perfect match.

She chose to see the good in her friend: Even when things began to go awry, Grace continued to think the best of her friend, for as long as she could. Grace had to begin lying to herself—not to mention her mom—in order to continue to view Ashley in this glorified light. However, *at least initially*, it is desirable for children to give their friends the benefit of the doubt in order to work out problems.

Applying the Four Steps: Strategies to use with your own daughter

STEP 1: OBSERVE

Notice contradictions: Grace's mom had seen some indications that the friendship with Ashley was not as positive as it once was. She had noticed that Grace was more and more the follower and was favoring playing with Ashley over any and all other kids. Requests for playdates with other children had disappeared, and invitations to birthday parties had dwindled. But Grace was also deliciously happy and sang Ashley's praises often enough that Mom had kept her nagging suspicions to herself. However, Grace increasingly began complaining about not feeling well and had been snapping at her siblings more readily. Although Mom had broached the topic of Ashley and her friendship a number of times, with Grace so loyal to her friend, Mom felt helpless to find out what might really have been going on behind the curtains her daughter had drawn around the friendship.

Without the benefit of the Four Steps, this situation sadly went on for almost two years. The toll it took on Grace and her whole family was immense. And while parents can do little to control destructive relationships or some of the situations children find themselves trapped within, there is a lot you can do to help them navigate away from or out of these friendships.

Pierce the shroud of secrecy: The protective secretiveness in Grace and Ashley's friendship is common in yo-yo friendships, where the victimized girl remains so loyal to her friend that even suspicious parents are locked out from hearing the true nature of what is going on, for a very long time. Often, the friendship had been so positive for so long, or continues to have so many positive interactions to balance out the negative ones, that the child continues to persist in her wishful notions of the friendship. Inevitably, the more powerful girl's need for control builds, and thus the incidents of cruelty become more common, more public, and/or more aggressive or obvious. It is sometimes only then that parents see enough to decide to intervene, or that the child herself reaches a point of such misery that she is able to view her yo-yo friendship with new perspective.

Sadly, these interactions can go on for a very long time, right under the noses of caring parents, in part because the powerful girl is often a really "nice girl" whom adults tend to like (at least initially), and because parents often lack the skills to see the signs and lack the knowledge to intervene. Grace's mom found herself in exactly this position—feeling unsure what might be true or not, knowing how likable and kind Ashley was overall, and, given Grace's loyalty, having no idea what to do.

Trust your instincts: With your newly trained Four-Step skills, you no doubt noticed some red flags already. Thus, observing that Grace, in general, had become more passive in her friendships, more isolated, and more protective, combined with noticing that she had been complaining of illness and had been harsher with her siblings, you have all you need to move forward in the process: form a connection and provide some guidance. Here again we say, "Trust your instincts." If your daughter says all is grand but you suspect differently, make a connection (or two, or three), and see where it leads you.

STEP 2: CONNECT

Take your time: The goal in connecting is to establish a framework of trust in which your child can open up and ultimately discover new insights into what she is feeling and thinking. If you move too quickly from observing to guiding, you lose the necessary connection that allows you to guide your child as part of a team. Grace's mom made this mistake: Instead of listening to Grace and working to understand the power of the hold Ashley had on her, Mom tried too quickly to get Grace to realize the ways Ashley was not a good friend. But without the connection between Mom and Grace, this backfired and Grace lied to protect her friend.

Set up a quiet moment: While sometimes life is a catch-as-catch-can sport, if you know you need to have a big heart-to-heart with your daughter, stack the deck in your favor. Choose a moment when you (and she) don't have to race off to the next activity, when the other children are otherwise engaged, and when she is in an emotionally neutral place.

Employ Active Listening, including empathy: First and foremost, you and your daughter need to become a team, and the only way to do that is for you to really see what it is that your child is being so loyal to, and why. In this scenario, Mom's job was to really hear what was going on for Grace. Thus, upon hearing the story of the decorated arms, as natural as it would be to feel annoyed, she might have said: "Wow. It is really important to you to stay connected with Ashley. You must feel like she's a really good friend." Once Grace had been able to establish *why* she felt this statement was true (and once Grace felt her mom was understanding her), Mom could have begun to ask some questions, to try and get more information *while staying connected.*

STEP 3: GUIDE

Identify the dual nature of the relationship: When you are able to establish a give-and-take rapport with your daughter (after you have fostered a connection), guide your child to recognize the two sides of her friendship—the side that feels really good, and the side that feels really awful (think about making a list of each). Holding dual emotions at the same time is a *real* challenge for children, and your daughter will need your guidance and support. Until girls begin to identify ("on their own") that the friendship has some serious limitations, it is extremely difficult to help them stand up for themselves, or to break away. Don't forget to draw on Active Listening and empathy as you guide your child. In this case, Mom could have said:

- ✧ "Yes, I really want to please my friends too. I think we all do. That's what good friends do—they each work at

the friendship to keep it equal. But I have been noticing that Ashley does less work to please *you*. It seems
like you are the one who is more often doing the extra
work in the friendship. Does it ever feel that way to
you?"

✥ "What do you do when you feel like you are doing more
of the work, or making more sacrifices than she is?"

Bolster her self-esteem: Part of why girls stay in yo-yo friendships
so long is that they lack self-esteem. Imagine saying things like,
"I am so proud of you for being a really good friend." Or, "I can
tell it makes you feel good to be so loyal. Ashley is lucky to have
a friend like you." Supportive statements like these can help her
build a sense of self-worth that may enable her to detach from
the relationship.

Take off the rose-colored glasses: Some of the wonderful qualities
many victims of yo-yo friendships possess are their immense
loyalty and their willingness to continue to give their friend the
benefit of the doubt, time and again. Part of guiding your child at
this point is to gently help her see that what she has continued to
label as friendship is actually manipulation. In Grace's case, Mom
could have commented, "Hmmm . . . I notice that Ashley has a
great deal of influence over the roles you take and the costumes you wear. I also notice that these costumes have gotten
you in trouble or left you feeling embarrassed. What have you
noticed?"

The goal of these types of conversations is to guide your child to realize that such situations are likely not a coincidence, but rather active manipulations by the powerful friend to assert her control over her too-loyal companion. It is only when you and your daughter are a team in facing this shattering reality that you can support and guide her to reclaim her own power and make more assertive choices moving forward. Don't be surprised if this takes a few interactions.

Make new friends . . . : Many girls stuck in yo-yo friendships become socially isolated and have few, if any, social options outside of their "best friend." Therefore, it is very important to support the extension of your daughter's friendship circle. This may feel impossible at first, so you may need to help her make connections with potential friends (see "Letting go of a friendship circle," on page 162).

Finding new friends was one idea that Grace's mom had suggested when the scope of the issue became clear to her. Unfortunately, as often happens when the passive girl in a yo-yo friendship tries to pull away, the other girl reasserts her power in more overt and distressing ways. In this situation, Grace tried to reestablish an old friendship with Stephanie. They had seemed to reconnect, but then Ashley said that Stephanie was making fun of Grace behind her back. This overt attempt to reclaim her place in Grace's life left Grace even more confused: Who was telling the truth, and whom could she trust?

Don't be surprised if this happens with your own child. The lure of control is immense for the powerful girl in yo-yo friendships, and she often won't let go without a fight. The trick here is to stay a team with your daughter. Go back to the Four Steps: Observe what is now going on, or the effects of what is going on, in your child's behavior. Connect with her again and create a safe space for her to identify feelings and thoughts as they arise. Then move forward to a new round of guiding and supporting to act. These more intense and complicated bully scenarios rarely resolve simply and painlessly. But when you and your child work together and follow the Steps, she is no longer alone to face these heartbreaking situations.

. . . but keep the old: It is the rare girl who will choose to abandon her intimate friendship immediately after she begins to realize the relationship has left her suffering. Unless your child is in a dangerous situation (in which case you should act immediately!), forcing the issue too early may drive a wedge between the two of you. Much as you might wish to remove this hurtful influence in your child's life, in all likelihood doing so will be a process. Talk to your daughter about ways you can help protect her with her friend, such as only having playdates at your house (under your supervision) for the time being, making the activities more structured (going for ice cream, doing an art project) or public (dancing to music in the family room as opposed to playing in the unsupervised basement).

Discuss the dangers of technology: In stark contrast to when we were younger, your child is growing up in a digital world. From cell phones to e-mails to video cameras to instant messaging, the influence of technology in your daughter's world is only a breath away, if you do not feel it already. Thus, girls need to know that whatever they do electronically is permanent, public, and—once in the hands of others—completely out of their control. Emphasize to your daughter that she should not do anything with a cell phone, computer, or video camera around that she does not want her best friend, her worst enemy, her mother, or her teacher to *also* see. No matter how good a friend might be today, you never know when she will do something "funny," like post a video or spam an e-mail.

Find support everywhere: In order for a victimized girl to more easily separate from her more powerful friend, it will help to have the twosome spend less time together, including being paired off less frequently in school. While Grace's mom may or may not have chosen to share the extent of the situation with Grace's teacher, she could certainly have told her something like, "Ashley and Grace had been having some social struggles

---

TEACHER'S Tip: Welcoming Parent Input

Welcome parent input whenever possible. The more parents feel they can share with you, the better you can do your job. One way to do this is to make your first response to every parent concern or comment, "I'm so glad you came to me with this." Bully situations this big often require a team approach, including the parents, you, and the school counselor.

lately and I think it would really help Grace if she could have some time away from being grouped with Ashley so often. Is there another child you might suggest who would be a good match?"

Find a way to separate the girls: If there is a vacation coming, or the end of the year is near, that is a perfect opportunity to help break the intensity of the friendship and to support your daughter to move in a new direction. In late spring, make a point to ask the teacher to have the girls be placed in different classes next year. Schools are usually receptive to this kind of request, even if they discourage parents from getting involved in class allocation choices. You are seeking a necessary and protective solution to an ongoing bullying situation. If you talk with the teacher or school counselor, the school will usually be happy to support your child in having an easier time next year.

STEP 4: SUPPORT TO ACT

Assertiveness training—dealing with girls at school: One tenet you will hear us come back to time and again is to help your daughter extricate herself from a negative interaction without adding fuel to the fire. Translated here, this means Grace needed support to pull away from Ashley without turning into a Mean Girl. So often, when really nice, sweet girls try to assert themselves, it takes everything they have to do so. The result is that they go too far the other way: speaking harshly, getting angry, drawing hard and fast lines. We talk about this in greater depth in chapter 6, but in order for Grace to have been able to assert herself without getting aggressive, she might have practiced these possibilities, said or done in a friendly way:

Choosing a new course of action:

- ❖ Smiling at Ashley, but choosing to sit beside a new friend at lunch.
- ❖ Inviting another girl to play with her and Ashley at recess.

Standing up for herself in a positive way:

- ❖ "I like your idea, Ashley, but I think we'd better find a costume from the materials Mrs. Kennedy gave us."
- ❖ "It would be really funny to wear a diaper, but if we're going to video it, I'd be more comfortable in my regular clothes. How about we add a rattle to the costume instead?"

Take advantage of the activities suggested throughout this guide:

- ❖ While virtually all of the activities in this book will benefit your daughter, some particularly relevant ones are: "Identifying manipulation in yo-yo friendships," on page 241, "What-if scenarios: yo-yo friendships," in appendix 2, on page 267, and "Assert yourself!," on page 88.

TEACHER'S Tip: Accomplishment Necklaces

As we mentioned, girls in yo-yo friendships often lack self-esteem. A nice activity to bolster self-esteem among all the members of the class is to make "accomplishment necklaces." Using Model Magic® clay, have your class make interesting-shaped flat beads, so they can write on them after they dry. Be sure to poke a hole in them to allow children to string beads into a "jewel" or "rock" necklace. Once dry, decorate the "jewels" or "rocks" and have students write a word on the back of each to remind them of something they do that they're proud of or good at (swimming, dance, singing, reading, etc.). Point out that these things that make us proud are as valuable as jewels or make us as strong as rocks. Tell your students that you will all wear your necklaces for the rest of the day to keep these treasures and strengths close to your hearts and to help you remember how special and important and wonderful each of them are. Think about having a "ceremony" before putting the necklaces on, where students share one word they wrote and why.

Support her strengths: You make it easier for your child to grow when you support her to do so in her area of strength. For instance, Grace loves theater. Mom could have signed Grace up for acting classes to help Grace meet girls who shared her interests, to extend her abilities in more positive ways, and to make it easier to pull away from Ashley.

Reclaim her power: As you have learned throughout this book, a lot of supporting your child to act involves helping your daughter to regain power. Only *she* can determine what she is ready to take on, but with you by her side, she may feel enabled to try new things. Think about investigating activities that will empower her, such as a children's self-defense course or a karate class. When a child feels brave and powerful in one area of her life, she is better able to bring these feelings and this sense of accomplishment to other areas.

Think about what might work for your child, and don't forget you can build on a skill she already possesses! Reyna's ten-year-old daughter, Natasha, has been fascinated by Irish dancing since preschool. She began taking lessons when she was six and had a knack for it. To help her become brave, Natasha began competing in Irish dance feises. While at first she was terrified to dance in front of hundreds of people, including judges, the reward of medals and trophies helped her muster the courage to do it. She was then able to carry this belief in her strengths and abilities to other aspects of life that she felt less confident about.

Blaming mom: Give your daughter permission to blame the break in the friendship on you. Invite her to say things like:

- ✿ "My mom, she is such a pain. She says I can only have sleepovers at my house. How about you sleep over here?"
- ✿ "Ugh! My mom says I have to play with more kids on the playground. How about we invite Stephanie to play our game with us today?"
- ✿ "I'm sorry I can't come over to play today. My mom is making me practice piano right after school."

Drawing the heavy hand: There may come a time when you feel you need to step in and help your daughter protect herself, as some situations are just too difficult for her to navigate on her own. If you find that despite her best efforts your daughter is unable to extricate herself from what has become an abusive or dangerous situation, you need to help her. This may mean setting up a meeting with school officials or drawing a hard and fast rule, such as telling your child she can no longer play with the other girl.

In this situation, Mom ultimately had to involve Grace's teacher in helping to keep the girls separate until the end of the year, and Mom insisted that the two be placed in separate classes the next year. She petitioned the school to know the names of a few girls who would be in Grace's class in the fall, so that the girls could begin building rapport over the summer. That summer, whenever Grace started talking about a playdate with Ashley, her mom reminded her of the need to break away, and then supported her to make a more positive choice.

Notably, Ashley never once called Grace to play, and by the fall, Grace had a few new friendships she was ready to strengthen at school. While she still spoke positively about the friendship and about missing its depth/intensity, she was able to move on and accept a newer, healthier balance of more (but less intimate) friends. These girls were better able to value Grace as a person and a friend. If this happens with your child, don't forget to draw on the Four Steps to observe, connect, guide, and support to act during this phase of adjustment. Be sure to offer a lot of positive support and encouragement for your daughter's bravery and integrity along the way.

Tips for Girls: When You Hear a Rumor About Yourself

When you hear people talking about you behind your back (or right in front of you!), it can send panic through you. It's easy to feel overwhelmed and to lose your sense of control and your feeling of power. But remember how to be assertive and remember your "I messages." And remember that you always have choices:

- Take some time to go over the Four Steps at home with a parent or other trusted adult. Make a plan.
- Think about who you have trusted with personal information. Most kids have trouble keeping a secret, and because best friends often change a lot in elementary school, you want to be very careful whom you tell your secrets to, and even more careful what kinds of personal information you share.
- Talk to the person who supposedly started the rumor. Use an "I statement" to:

  - Tell her what you heard
  - Tell her how it made you feel
  - Tell her what you want her to do.

For example, you might say, "I heard there is a rumor going around about me. I don't know who started it, but I'm upset about it because it's not true/it's embarrassing/etc. If you've heard this rumor, please don't spread it." Notice that you *don't* have to ask the other person if she is the one who spread the rumor (which may just make her defensive). You can just tell her what you heard and ask her to please stop.

**When someone starts saying untrue or unkind things
about you in front of you:**

- You always have the choice to walk away.
- Use "I statements" to assert yourself without being mean.
- Look bored—not scared or hurt or angry. Reclaim your power (think of mismatched barrettes; see page 134), and find an alternative activity or different people to be with.
- Ask the person, "Can you give me an example?" Naming specifics refocuses the discussion to one-on-one relationships, as opposed to people talking in generalities.
- If this is not true, remind yourself and others, "I know what is true and not true. And I know that is not true."
- If it is true, remind yourself (or the other person), "OK, that's your opinion."
- Lighten the situation: Crack a joke or poke fun at yourself.

5

Going Along with the Gang

While some girls will always gravitate toward a single, intense friendship, most will find themselves vacillating between "best friends" and group friendships, with many pairs of best friends coexisting within friendship circles. In early elementary school, these friendship groups will ebb and flow, and girls will move freely among them. However, as girls age, these circles often become cliques, and breaking in to one becomes more challenging.

The benefit to having a circle of friends is that your daughter knows there is a group of people who share similar interests, who know her well, and who can provide support and companionship. The downside is that groups can also create rules or standards that make some of the members fear being excluded or "ousted." In fact, it is a rare group that survives an entire school year without struggle and upset. Often, within a group, girls are asked to take sides in various arguments, informally determine group leadership, and show loyalty to the group above any individual member. This loyalty may include being "forced" to conform or to oust nonconforming members. No wonder girls can feel overwhelmed or stressed about going to school! In the coming pages, we examine the challenges girls face regarding group membership, and how to manage the inevitable group struggles that can rock the foundation of confidence girls feel.

When Girls Struggle to Fit In

This story highlights the struggles children go through when they are trying to fit in to school culture. The suggestions apply to scenarios where children are panicked about doing "it" (whatever "it" is) just right.

Crazy Sock Day

Amelia waved the notice as she told her mom, excitedly, "Tomorrow is Crazy Sock Day. It's a school spirit thing—I'm supposed to wear crazy socks." Her mother placed the notice on the counter on her way to the fridge. "What flavor yogurt would you like this afternoon?" she asked her five-year-old kindergartener. "Strawberry . . . Didn't you hear what I said?" Amelia asked flatly. "Tomorrow is Crazy Sock Day. There are signs all around the school. I heard the fourth graders talking about it in the hall. I have to wear crazy socks. I have the striped ones, but those might be too crazy." "What about the ones with the kitties on them," her mother offered, "those are cute." "Cute? I said they had to be crazy. What if I can't find any? What if I choose the wrong ones? What if my friends laugh at the socks I choose? Can we go to the store?" "Go to the store to buy crazy socks?" her mother questioned, "I think the striped ones will be fine." Amelia, obviously upset, shouted, "No! I told you those are too crazy! Everyone is going to have *good* crazy socks to wear tomorrow; I have to have good ones too!" With that, Amelia stormed upstairs and slammed her door. She dumped out her socks on the floor. "All these socks are wrong!" she shouted, collapsing in a fit of tears. Amelia's mom listened at the door, dumbstruck that her daughter could be in such an hysterical state over something as ridiculous as crazy socks.

What happened and why?

With girls' entrance into elementary school comes a newfound awareness of themselves as members of social communities outside their family. Despite the fact that a great majority of children attend preschool, it is not until kindergarten that they are cognitively capable of recognizing themselves as participants in *cultural communities* outside their homes. Children are consistently aware of the grades above and below them—of exactly where they fit in the social hierarchy. Thus, for the first time, Amelia realizes that she can be an accepted *or rejected* member of her school community. Not surprisingly, with this realization comes Amelia's desire to fit in and be accepted by her peers and classmates.

What Amelia did well

She recognized that she wanted to be part of the school social scene: Amelia is now old enough to recognize that she is one of the youngest members of the community known as school. She

longs to fit in and to be part of the group, and hearing older children talk about Crazy Sock Day only confirmed to her the importance of wearing "cool" crazy socks in order to belong.

She actively sought to connect with her mom around a social issue: Isn't this what you always hope for as a parent—to have your child come home and announce loud and clear that she is facing a struggle and seeking support? In fact, Amelia stated multiple times exactly what she (thought) she needed: a pair of really good crazy socks to wear to school.

Applying the Four Steps: Strategies to use with your own daughter

Amelia's mom didn't have the benefit of the Four Steps, and so she and Amelia remained at odds over the absurdity of worrying about crazy socks. Amelia alternated between being angry and withdrawn the rest of the night. She reluctantly wore a pair of mismatched socks. After school, Mom asked Amelia how it went and felt a twinge of satisfaction that it had really not been as bad as Amelia had assumed it would be. Unfortunately, while Amelia got over the sock incident, an important opportunity was lost. Had Mom had the Four Steps to draw on, she could have helped Amelia face Crazy Sock Day with greater confidence, and she would have had the opportunity to learn about the "real" issue behind the worry over socks. Mom also would have been able to foster Amelia's skills and resiliency for future struggles, as well as to deepen the base of support between them in facing these types of social issues as a team. Let's walk through what the Four Steps would have looked like in this scenario.

STEP 1: OBSERVE

Notice what she shows you: Amelia made observing easy: she walked in the door and announced her need for a pair of crazy socks. While it may seem that Mom was then ready to move on to connecting, the door was open to invest in a bit of observational reflecting. If your child comes to you with a similar concern, try to think about the larger context of these social issues. This will help you better connect with and guide your daughter. So take a minute in the heat of the moment to try to contextualize your daughter's struggle.

In this case, Mom could have remembered that Amelia was coming off a botched playdate, where she and her friend had gotten into an argument over who had the better Littlest Pet Shop™ collection. Mom had needed to intervene and set up a structured art project to help the girls reconnect, but even that had been tenuous. Realizing this, Mom would have been in a better place to understand her daughter's sense of urgency and to more effectively connect, guide, and support Amelia to act.

STEP 2: CONNECT

Once you realize the extent of the situation, you are ready to connect fully with your child. The goal is to give your daughter the space to experience her feelings with a loving, listening partner—one who will reflect back *without judging* and will take note *without racing in to fix things*. Regardless of how the interaction has gone thus far, there is always room to come back and connect with your child and start anew.

Make physical contact and slow things down: Amelia's mom could have changed the dynamic instantly if she had scooped up her distraught daughter and snuggled with her. Especially for young girls, physical proximity helps to slow breathing and allow thoughts to stop racing. With a calm head and a warmed heart, Amelia would have been ready to reconnect.

Admit you may not have been ready to listen before: Amelia's mom handled the situation as most of us would—she causally put aside a school notice about something of seeming little importance and tried to move the afternoon along. It became clear that Amelia needed something different, and once she stormed off, the door was open for Mom to reflect on what her next steps could have been. When this happens in your home, reapproach your daughter using the Four Steps.

With Amelia calming down in her arms, Mom could have reopened discussion with Active Listening, saying something like, "I wasn't really hearing what you were saying downstairs. Can I try again? It sounds like it's pretty important to find a just-right pair of crazy socks for tomorrow, and you're worried that the ones we have will be too crazy." These types of reflective statements let your child know you heard her, make room for her to correct you if necessary, and encourage her to further expand on what she is feeling or thinking.

Extend Active Listening, including empathy: The goal in this interaction is to encourage whatever feelings your child has been holding to be released, so that they can better inform how you—the loving parent—can guide and support her. If Amelia's mom had continued to draw on Active Listening, she would have discovered that kids in Amelia's class had made fun of some of the clothes of another girl in the class. Amelia was extremely worried that if she wore the wrong socks, her friends would make fun of her too.

Once you fully understand where your child's emotions are coming from, you can empathize with her. Here, Amelia's mom could have stroked her hair and told her lovingly, "Wow. I can imagine you would feel really scared to go to school, worrying

---

TEACHER'S Tip: School Spirit Days

School or team spirit days (for example, Broncos Jersey Mondays) can be great fun for your class. However, you will want to remain sensitive to children who do not or cannot participate. If you notice (observe) a child who seems to be hanging back on these days, make a point of going over and connecting with her around a topic of interest. Let her know what a valuable member of the group you feel she is. When children feel disconnected from school, a teacher's comments and efforts to include them are often all they need to feel like true members of the class community again!

that wearing the wrong socks would make your friends laugh at you. You are really brave to think so carefully about finding a pair that you will be confident to wear."

STEP 3: GUIDE

Once you have observed the problem and connected with your daughter, you are ready to provide guidance. As we have mentioned, doing so will allow her to discover the options *she* has in a situation, even if she cannot control what *her friends* might do.

Identify the real issue: Sometimes children focus on one aspect of a problem, when the real issue is something else entirely. Through observing and connecting, you are likely to discover what is really going on. Once you know this, you can better guide her. Without the Four Steps, Mom felt her role was to give Amelia a "reality check" and convince her that she was worrying about nothing. However, because Mom jumped from what she saw as the problem (the worry about socks) to what she saw as the solution (having a reality check on the worry's importance), she missed the true issue: Amelia's sense of vulnerability around her friends.

Thus, when you effectively observe and connect, you can help your child identify where her feelings of worry or anxiety are actually coming from. In this case, if Mom had the benefit of the Four Steps, she could have addressed Amelia's two fears at the same time: "Sounds like you have a lot you are worrying about:

finding the right socks *and* staying connected to your friends. So let's see what ideas we can come up with to figure out both of these problems, okay?"

Brainstorm a series of possibilities: From there, Mom and Amelia could have worked as a team to brainstorm a list of possible solutions. As we mentioned previously, embrace any and all suggestions at this stage, and whittle down your list to only those you both are willing and able to follow through on *after* her participation has been fully welcomed. As always, you should add your own more realistic suggestions as well.

Scale the worry down to size: Social situations often feel really big, even if in reality they are not. Thus, girls sometimes need a loving guide to help them see that some worries *seem* bigger than they actually are. Your child is experiencing a very real fear or worry; be respectful of that. Help her understand that *some worries* (like her worry about the socks) *get smaller as they are faced.* Try the mismatched barrettes activity (see box) for ways your child can better manage the unkind things children sometimes say.

If Mom had had the benefit of the Four Steps, she might have said, "Amelia, I know you are really worried about finding the right socks to wear, and that it feels like something really bad might happen if you don't. And I want to help you keep this worry in a box that is the right size. Right now, you are keeping it in a very big box (mime holding a really big box that sort of makes you lose your balance). Your sock worry doesn't need such a big box, so let's get it a smaller box (mime a much smaller box that you can comfortably hold). When we find just the right size box for the problem, we can see the worry at its real size, and you can be less overwhelmed, not having to carry around such a too-big worry box."

Tips for Girls: Mismatched Barrettes

Sometimes, when you hear things people say, or stand by watching as they exclude you or hurt your feelings, your heart races and your chest tightens. It can feel like your power is slipping away. One way to help combat those feelings is to counter them with some calming thoughts.

For some people, this is thinking about running water, or far-away beaches. In Michelle's house, we say, "It's just like they told me I am wearing mismatched barrettes. Really, who cares? It's nothing to be upset about. Just because they are upset about mismatched barrettes doesn't mean I have to be."

If you can find a way to think "who cares?" *and believe it*, your reaction, your body language, and your tone of voice will be more relaxed. In keeping yourself centered and calm, you take away the Mean Girl's power because she hasn't zapped you of yours.

Have your parents tell you Amelia's story. Imagine you are trying to help Amelia. How can you help her use the mismatched barrettes strategy to feel better about her worry that her friends will make fun of her if her socks are too crazy?

Help your child identify both issues: Most girls will struggle with how to manage friendships for many years. Thus, every time a new but similar issue arises, it gives you the opportunity to help your child extend current skills and develop new ones. Through the Four-Step process, we learned that behind Amelia's sock worry was a friend worry. Thus, part of *guiding* her would have been helping her consider how to strengthen social connections with friends. Be sure you and your daughter take advantage of all the resources available to you in the "Think, Share, Do . . ." chapters!

STEP 4: SUPPORT TO ACT

Once you have had a chance to talk about and strategize a solution to the issue(s) your daughter is facing, you are ready to support her to act. Some girls are ready and eager at this stage to make a plan and follow it through, while others are more hesitant. Remember that your goal is to support your child as she prepares to act *on her own behalf.* If that involves baby steps or waiting longer than you wish to take the first step, consider it all a part of the learning curve.

Set realistic parameters: Supporting your daughter socially does not mean opening your pocketbook or jumping every time she feels she needs something new in order to fit in. Be honest with your child in terms of what is possible. Even if you are not opposed to buying some fun crazy socks, you may not be able to do so by tomorrow. When you are honest in a loving and supportive way, you may be surprised at how inventive your child can be (with your support) in solving her own problem creatively! For example, one day, eight-year-old Kylie was working on an end-of-unit school project. However, it turned out there was not enough poster board to cover her castle in stones. Kylie was distraught that Michelle was not able to go out and buy more poster board. But necessity is the mother of invention, and when Kylie got over her disappointment, she decided to cover the stoneless side with real ivy Michelle glue-gunned on. Both she and her classmates loved the effect of the ivy even better than the stones.

Become a team: While your daughter might be disappointed that you are "refusing to help her" follow through on what she sees as the necessary solution (going store-to-store to find the perfect socks, right now), you can still remain a team. Empathizing can help: "Amelia, I see how disappointed you are that we can't buy new socks for Crazy Sock Day tomorrow. I would be disappointed too. But we are a team, and you and I will figure this out together. Let's look at some of the other ideas on our list and see what might work, even if it's not perfect."

Find a solution she can live with and feel comfortable about: The reality is, you and your child may not find the perfect solution that is realistic, doable, will fix everything, and can make everybody happy. Instead, there are solutions that will work for *right now*, and there are those that can be built on *for the future*. So for right now she can:

- ❖ Call a friend to borrow fun socks
- ❖ Combine a funny/mismatched pair in the drawer she has
- ❖ Cope with deciding not to wear crazy socks by wearing long pants and boots, so no one will know whether or not she has socks on at all

❖ Decide to manage possible social rejection by practicing saying, "It's Crazy Sock Day? I had no idea. But, wow, I really like *your* socks!" in a casual, friendly way

What she decides is unimportant, as long as she feels good about it, and as long as she knows she has you to help her problem solve.

TEACHER'S Tip: Showing School Spirit

School (or team) spirit days are meant to be a way for children to connect with and feel positive about the school community as a whole. Emphasize this larger meaning in your class. Have the children brainstorm a list of ways they show school spirit every day. Help them remember that even if they do not (or cannot) participate in a specific spirit activity, they can still contribute to the larger purpose of the event by continuing to show spirit on their own!

Plan ahead: Children get mired in the immediate problem and its sense of urgency. Rather than move from emergency to emergency, take a moment to invest in an ounce of prevention. Solutions that can be built on for the future include looking ahead in the school calendar to find other special days, and brainstorming together to decide what she may like to plan for those days. Remember to couch this in terms of the two of you acting as a team to face the future together! Not only will this save both of you a lot of heartache, it will help mitigate any disappointment she may feel at not having the perfect solution to this "right now" crisis.

Strengthen friendships: Helping children keep and strengthen relationships with friends is a theme you will see time and again in this book. When the immediacy of Crazy Sock Day has passed, see the activities in the "Think, Share, Do . . ." chapters for ideas on how to help your child strengthen and expand her friendships.

When Girls Struggle with Feeling "Different"

This story highlights the struggles children go through when they feel different. The strategies deal with a visible difference (race, ethnicity, physical disability, and so on). The strategies also apply to a more hidden difference (religion, learning differences, differences in family structure such as divorce, and so on).

Do Whispers Mean Trouble?

Carley is an outgoing biracial second grader who speaks Japanese (her mother's native language) at home. Carley loves it when Mom comes to eat lunch with her at school. One Tuesday in early November, Carley's mom arrived just as Carley and her best friend, Jordan, began planning what to play together at recess. To help her mother fit at the table, Carley squeezed close to another girl and introduced Jordan to her mom. Carley thought she saw Jordan's smile diminish. Jordan shifted in her seat when Carley and her mom started chatting in Japanese.

Suddenly, Jordan took her tray and politely excused herself, saying, "It will be more comfortable if the table isn't so squished," before walking over to go sit with Julia at a nearby table. Carley noticed that a number of her other friends coming out of the hot lunch line went to sit with Jordan and Julia. She saw Jordan whispering to Julia, and she swore she saw them stealing glances at her and her mom. When Carley saw them laugh, she was certain they were talking about her. She privately begged her mom to take her to the library for recess. That evening, Carley told her mom she knew Jordan was whispering to Julia about her at lunch. She burst into tears, saying, "I saw her talking to the other girls about me as well. They're all making fun of me. I can't go to school tomorrow. Please don't make me!"

What happened and why?

It can happen to any girl at any time: the plunge from complete confidence to total despair, from a sense of pride to one of humiliation, from feeling competent to feeling inept. And there is no more certain cause than what your child perceives as a judgment from a friend or an exclusion from a group. For girls this age, fitting in and being seen as "one of the gang" is imperative. Thus, when Carley noticed her friend pull away during lunch and then surround herself with other girls, she was sure they must have been talking about her. By this simple move alone, Carley feared she was ousted from the group. And with the "you're in or you're out" mentality of many groups, Carley knew that being ousted could have significant social repercussions.

What Carley did well

She removed herself from what she felt was an unsafe situation: Carley perceived the environment to be unsafe, so she wisely found a way to remove herself (by asking her mom to take her to the library for recess). It is empowering for children to feel they have ways to protect themselves in what seem (to them) to be unsafe interactions. This may be as simple as asking to go to the bathroom, seeking a pass to the library, finding a set of other people to interact with, or having a "play alone" plan they can pull out in times of need. Of course, we strongly advise connecting with and guiding your child so that she can better distinguish an uncomfortable situation such as this from a truly dangerous one.

She didn't lose it at lunch: When children are in preschool, temper tantrums and outbursts of sadness and anger are common. But by kindergarten, the number and intensity of these explosions are in decline. This occurs in part because children's moods are more stable as they mature, and in part because children know they will suffer social stigma and be seen as "babies" if they cry too often in front of their peers. Despite being extremely upset, Carley was able to hold it together and remove herself from the situation before she broke down.

She sought her mom's involvement: While her mom was at lunch, she did not notice Carley's change in affect after Jordan left. However, that evening, Carley was able to approach her mom and let her know she was in need of connection and support.

Applying the Four Steps: Strategies to use with your own daughter

STEPS 1 & 2: OBSERVE AND CONNECT

Two birds with one stone: Like Amelia, Carley made one aspect of observing easy: She announced her need for parental involvement. What remained hidden was exactly what was contributing to the assumptions Carley made about Jordan. Here is where observing and connecting go hand-in-hand. By Actively Listening and asking Carley good questions, Mom could discover what may have been going on below the surface, contributing to Carley's sense of panic.

By listening without judging that evening, Mom helped Carley open up. "My friends think being Japanese is strange," Carley confided, somewhat embarrassed. "I've seen them sometimes do the slanty eye thing when they think I'm not around. It makes me really mad. It's not like I'm *really* Japanese or anything." Carley's mom was stunned, enraged, and confused. She had to swallow her outrage to stay present with her daughter's desire to fit in and be like her friends. "It's hard for you to be different," she mustered. "Sometimes you wish you could erase the parts of you that make you stand out from your friends." You could see relief in Carley's face: her mom wasn't mad like she thought she would be—she *understood*. A weight was lifted off Carley's shoulders and she felt closer to her mom than ever. Carley was open to guidance in a whole new way.

STEP 3: GUIDE

Depersonalize the situation and present alternative perspectives: Girls need help to see that not all situations are black and white; in fact, most are various shades of gray. In addition, they need to know that their parents will remain their allies without getting so involved that it feels like the world is ending. As Dr. Michael Thompson says, you do not want to be continually "interviewing for pain," because that is often exactly what you will find. However, at the same time, girls need to feel their worries and concerns are important enough to matter, or they are likely to push them underground. As research from the Ophelia Project reports, thinking your problem is too small to matter or holding your feelings inside rarely works in the long run, and often leaves girls unavailable for learning. Carley was convinced that her friend Jordan left the lunch table because she felt uncomfortable around Carley's mom, because she was Asian, looked different, and spoke Japanese. While of course this was possible, it was just as likely Jordan left because of the wonderful connection Carley and her mom were sharing, having an animated conversation in Japanese, where *Jordan* was the one actually feeling left out.

Mom could also help Carley realize that the whispers she saw may not have been due to a desire of Jordan's to make fun of Carley. Instead, they may have been due to the fact that Jordan was confiding in Julia about being uncomfortable feeling left out of the interaction—or other things. The goal here is not to convince your child that she is wrong in her assessment, or that you know better. Instead, try to open her up to the *possibility* of more than one interpretation of the events.

Tips for Girls: Whispers, Rumors, and Secrets

To help you think more about whispers, rumors, secrets, and the effect they can have on decisions you make or how you feel about yourself or others, read *Snail Started It!*, by Katja Reider and Angela Von Roehl, and *Help!: A Story of Friendship,* by Holly Keller. Ask your parents to tell you Carley's story. What might you say to Carley in the lunchroom? How might you approach Jordan?

Develop her sense of cultural pride: It is possible the girls were making fun of Carley for having Japanese heritage. Sadly, this is an all-too-common experience for many children, regardless of what that difference might be (race, culture, learning abilities, religion, style of dress). In Carley's case, she was one of the few children of color at her school, and thus when she looked around, she felt that she was noticeably different in an obvious way from her peers. To her (at the moment) this difference was bad. Mom could help Carley feel pride in her heritage by finding community connections outside of school where she could connect with other Japanese children, or children from biracial families.

Identifying with your child's struggle around issues of acceptance and identity alleviates her sense of alienation. Reyna's family decided to join a temple for just this reason: then eight-year-old Natasha was one of the only Jewish children in her entire elementary school, which sometimes left her feeling alone among her friends. To help Natasha find people with similar experiences, Reyna found not only a synagogue but also a like-minded community.

Stop the rumor mill: There is nothing worse than a she-said, she-said situation that escalates because each party is making assumptions. Given the number of times girls end up reacting to hear-say and rumors, it is important to instill in your daughter an ethos to interact around the problem with the actual girl involved—see "Gossip and Rumors" and "Whispers, Rumors, and Secrets" (boxes) for more on how your daughter can approach these issues. While this is not easy, especially at the beginning, we promise that playing the guessing game and assuming the worst will get neither of you anywhere!

TEACHER'S Tip: Visual Rumors

Try out this visual activity to help your students better understand what happens when people spread rumors: Get a bin full of small items (Unifix cubes, jewels, beads). You will need to collect any stray items at the end, so choose items that are easily swept up. Tape the word "the truth" on one item. Explain to your students that the beads are like rumors. Tell your students to watch them carefully—they need to keep track of where these "rumors" are spreading. Then, in a large space, toss the beads everywhere. Instruct your students to collect the "rumors" and to find the one bead with "the truth." After they have collected as many as possible, see if anyone found "the truth." Sometimes they will and sometimes they won't, but it sure isn't easy to find! Point out that spreading rumors or passing on gossip is like throwing beads: You don't decide where things fly, and once it leaves your mouth, you no longer control who says what to whom. Comment that often it is impossible to find the truth in a rumor.

Tips for Girls: Gossip and Rumors

Spreading rumors is like throwing confetti into the wind: You don't control where the pieces fly, and no matter how hard you might try, you'll never be able to get them all back. Regardless of whether what you share is true, once it leaves your mouth, you no longer control who says what to whom. While it's a natural thing to do, when you listen to rumors and gossip, or pass them on, you are acting like a Mean Girl, however unintentionally. Be a good friend and remember, private is private. So what can you do instead? Answer some questions in your mind:

- Why do I want to listen to this story?
- How will it make me feel to join in or to pass it on?
- Would I want people to know this about me? Say these things about me?

Your answers will help you figure out the best thing to do.

What can you do?

- Imagine your friend's face when she hears what you have been saying.
- Say to the person telling you the rumor, "Can I quote you on this?"
- Stand up for the person being gossiped about: "You know, what I like most about _____ is . . ."
- Clarify if it is true or not: "Have you talked to _____ about this?"
- Work to fix the problem or address the issue directly.

For example, Faith tells you that Amy said she doesn't want to sit with you at lunch anymore. What can you do? Remember, the goal is *not* to be aggressive, or to try to get Faith in trouble with Amy, or get Amy to admit what she might have said.

Instead, you want to be assertive in addressing the real issue by saying something like: "Amy, I heard that you don't want to sit with me at lunch. I felt sad when I heard that. If you don't want to sit with me, I'd like us to talk about that." Even if Amy did not start the rumor, giving her the opportunity to talk about it will let the two of you try to fix your friendship. Listen to Amy's concerns, use I statements (see page 91), and draw on the three Rs" (see page 207) if you inadvertently did something to hurt Amy's feelings.

Notice that you don't need to ask your friend if she started the rumor—that will likely make her feel defensive. If the goal is to talk about *why* she doesn't want to sit with you at lunch, talk about that and don't get distracted trying to "prove" that your friend was talking behind your back.

STEP 4: SUPPORT TO ACT

Bring her culture to school with her: There is not a school in this country that does not celebrate diversity as a central tenet. How well these goals are actualized is another matter, but if you approach the school with some ideas for bringing your culture into the classroom in a positive way, you are almost guaranteed to be met with enthusiasm. Some ideas to think about:

✿ Celebrate a holiday specific to your cultural or religious group. In Carley's case, this could be Japanese Girls'

Day (called hina-matsuri, "Japanese doll festival"), celebrated on March 3. Carley's mom might have organized a celebration of this festive day at school. Or, she
could have planned an at-home celebration with classmates.

✤ Bring in a familiar story (such as *The Very Hungry Caterpillar*, by Eric Carle) in your family's native language
(libraries have books in different languages). In this
case, Carley's mom encouraged Carley's classmates to
become detectives: Could they figure out the word for
sun, apple, or caterpillar in Japanese?

TEACHER'S Tip: Multicultural Reading

Although it is wonderful to have a native speaker actually read the
book, *teachers* can also do this activity to enhance a celebration of differences (read a book or play a story CD that is read in more than one
language, for example), without needing to involve a specific child or
her family. Don't worry about your accent—make it part of the learning experience for *all* of you!

✤ Offer to volunteer in your daughter's class to bring aspects of your culture's or religion's art or music to
school. Here Carley's mom could have come in to demonstrate to the children how to use simple brushstrokes
to produce beautiful art in the style of traditional Japanese drawings.

❖ Think of a way to incorporate pop culture. Carley's family had recently been to Epcot theme park at Walt Disney World. While there, they had shopped at the Japan Pavilion market. Bringing in these items from Disney World was a huge hit with Carley's class! If you are planning a trip, think about bringing back inexpensive "cultural souvenirs" (an interesting coin or small figurine) for each of your daughter's classmates (if this is permitted), or a wall hanging for the teacher to display.

TEACHER'S Tip: Go Fish

Simple games like Go Fish can help your students learn that even if we seem alike, we are *all* different, and that's a good thing! Use a regular deck of cards, and let your students play until every child has at least one set of four (even if she has to "trade" with a game mate to make a set). Students should then put their set faceup. Ask your students: What makes it a set? (Being the same number.) Encourage your students to look closely: How are the cards different? (Color or shape/suit.) Comment that we can think of our sets as groups of people that have something in common, like being part of a group that likes to jump rope. Even though we all are alike in that we like to jump rope, we are also all different in other ways that may not be obvious at first. We all are unique, just like all of the cards in our sets are unique. Next, have your students think about a group they are part of—a team, an after-school class, a street. Write their ideas on the board, and ask them about the groups they belong to, how the members are different, and how those differences make the group better.

Notice and support the ways kids can feel "different": Children often feel like "outsiders" (or are made to *feel* like outsiders) for a variety of differences—learning style, family structure, religion, even clothing choice! For example, some girls may dress or act less "girly" than the norm, which can leave them vulnerable to the "gender rules" children often enforce, from as young as kindergarten!

TEACHER'S Tip: De-Stereotyping Colors

If you notice a girl who is being picked on or left out because of the clothing she wears, try doing a project where kids need to think of why various colors are so special. Support a less gender-based division of ideas (green is like nature, yellow is like sunshine, pink is like flowers, and so forth) to celebrate how all colors are special and all colors can be for all kids, if they want them to be. Point out when teachers wear colors in nontypecast ways (for example, when a male teacher wears a pink shirt), or solicit colleagues to break stereotypes at various points. You could also have a "wear green day" (for example) for everyone in the class, or ask the children to wear a favorite shirt and bring something in to go with it that helps explain why it is a favorite, moving them past gender stereotypes.

Make a casual connection: The interaction between Carley and Jordan somehow turned intense. The girls did not have a falling-out per se, so the ground was still there for reconnecting. Carley decided to make Jordan a friendship bracelet that evening and gave it to her on the way into school. Jordan proudly wore it all day, and the two played nonstop at recess together with Julia and the other girls, the incident completely forgotten.

When Girls Struggle with Going Along with the Group

This story highlights the struggles children go through when going along with the group means going against themselves. The suggestions apply to scenarios where children are worried about needing to act in a way that is uncomfortable to them in order to participate in group activities.

Playing Dare

Sachi, Dana, Nyssa, Fiona, and Belle have been friends since the beginning of the year. As fourth graders, they now have recess on a different playground than the younger children, with only one teacher's aide instead of two. Dana tells us,

"It's because we're older and more responsible."

"What do *you* think of the new playground?" we ask Fiona, who is hanging back, as the others go in after recess.

"Uh. It's fine, I guess. Dana really likes that we can do pretty much what we want without anyone interrupting us or seeing us."

"What kinds of things does Dana like to do?"

"Things like Dare, where one of us has to do the dares the group gives us. Dana made up that game, but I really don't like it. I mean, I want to play with them. I just wish they wouldn't play games like that. Last week, we were sitting on the bench at recess, and everyone wanted to play Dare. So they were coming up with funny dares—like having Sachi run through the boys' wall ball game, or daring Nyssa to run up to a fifth-grade boy and say hi. Then they dared me to go sit on the wet, dirty bench *without* sitting on my jacket. I'm like, no way! Dana kept saying that if I wanted to play with them, I had to. So I went and sat on the bench *on* my jacket and Sachi jumped all over me—telling me that I wasn't playing fair and I had to *not* sit on my jacket. But I told them I would only do it *on* my jacket. They told me I couldn't play the game anymore, because I wasn't following the rules. I really didn't have anyone else to play with, and they're my friends, so I sort of hung out and watched. They thought it was okay that I was there, but they didn't include me in the game anymore."

What happened and why?

Beginning around the age of eight, girls form more consistent groups and friendships. They may not have a permanent best friend, instead continuing with what Dr. JoAnne Deak calls "Baskin-Robbins Friendships." This means that girls are still trying out various flavors to see which ones they like best. However, chances are, they are beginning to narrow it down to a select handful. Around third grade, all children (boys as well as girls) long to be part of something bigger than themselves, and they want to do it with friends. Suddenly, whom your daughter sits with at lunch, or whom she partners with in math class, really matters.

Elementary-aged children begin relating with peers according to conventions, and play moves from free-form and amorphic to being elaborately structured by rules. Children take these rules literally and seriously: If you want to play the game, you need to adhere to them. According to Dr. Michael Thompson, in *Best Friends, Worst Enemies*, being present and participating in group activity takes on increased importance for children in later elementary school: "[Children] show off to each other and they coach each other." In this way, there is less room for "doing it your own way" or going against the group, if you want to maintain membership.

What Fiona did well

She attempted to participate at her comfort level: Fiona wanted to be part of the group, which virtually all girls do, but she did not like the game they had chosen. Rather than give in or stomp off, she attempted to modify the rules. Notice that she did not ask for permission to do this. Sometimes, talking things out can backfire. If Fiona had asked "permission" to break the rule, she would surely have met with a chorus of resistance. After the action was finished, the group responded similarly, but Fiona had also *already* met *part* of the group's requirement for participation. This made it easier for the group to ultimately move on to the next girl's dare without subjecting Fiona to sustained backlash.

She stood her ground: Fiona did something that is increasingly hard for young girls to do: she stood her ground against the group. Consider it a small victory that will add up to bigger ones. When a girl is able to assert herself in little ways, the group learns her individual limits. Over time, the pressure on this girl is lessened, because the group has seen her stand up for herself. Rather than be in a position of causing open conflict, which many group members this age still attempt to avoid, group leaders will choose *not* to push these "stronger" girls the way they push "weaker" ones.

She remained nearby to be present without participating: Even though Fiona was kicked out of the next rounds of Dare, it was clear that she was still a member of the group. One way Fiona was able to maintain group membership was by remaining present during the activities, even those she did not participate in. This allowed her to take part in group memories, keep up with social dialogue ("Remember when Sachi ran through the wall ball game and got hit by the ball?"), and make continued choices about when she wanted to try to reenter the play. While she was obviously not happy about what had happened, by "hovering nearby" but not participating, she preserved the possibility of future group membership, and maintained her self-esteem.

Applying the Four-Steps: Strategies to use with your own daughter

STEP 1: OBSERVE

Find an opening for discussions both "big" and "small": In order for you to be able to help guide your daughter—and therefore help her expand her arsenal of choices or support—you need her to tell you social stories. Here, it was only when mom noticed Fiona's ruined jacket that the topic came up. A goal of this book is to help your child feel like she can (and would want to) come to you with both "small" and "big" social problems.

One way to do this is to notice when your daughter attempts to open a dialogue about friendship issues, even if it is indirectly. For example, Fiona off-handedly commented to her mother that now there was only one teacher's aide on the playground. It is important that parents lay the groundwork necessary to encourage girls to share these seemingly innocent and off-hand conversation-starters (because opportunities to connect and guide are often hidden in them!). Follow up with Active Listening, fostering the connection between you and your daughter.

Observe your child's ability to stand up to her friends: Listen to (observe) stories your daughter reports. Is she someone the group members know they can push around more, or is she someone who has been winning small victories like Fiona's, and thus will likely face fewer group challenges for the next few years? While standing one's ground is risky (the group could in fact oust girls like Fiona, or choose to take them on as they get closer to middle school), the benefits of building this type of "backbone" during elementary school are immense. Girls who are able to stand up for themselves are less likely to fall prey to peer pressure.

STEP 2: CONNECT

Congratulate her on a job well done!: As you know, it is extremely hard to stand up to a group of people you care about, even as an

> ## Tips for Girls: Take a Stand for a Friend
>
> In this story, Fiona is very brave about standing up for herself.
> Sometimes it can feel hard to stand up for yourself! One way to prac-
> tice is to stand up for a friend! Remind yourself about "I state-
> ments" (see page 91) and how to speak assertively without being
> mean (which will only start or continue the fight and in the end won't
> really help anyone), and help out a friend! Five-year-old Maya found
> she made a new connection when she saw a girl in her class being
> excluded by her friend Courtney. Maya went up to Courtney and
> said, "Isabel wants to play with you and you are ignoring her. Let's
> find a way we can all play!" When she came home to tell Michelle
> about it she said, "Mom, I didn't know how good *I* would feel helping
> *her* feel good! Now I have a new friend I can play with at recess!" So
> next time you see someone being left out, take a stand, and notice
> how great *you* feel as a result!

adult. What Fiona did was remarkable. She stood her ground
with a group of friends and found a way to participate without
compromising herself, or going beyond her comfort level. Letting your daughter know how proud you are of her strength of
character will help bolster her belief in herself and her willingness to stand up for herself, especially when she knows you are
standing firmly in her corner.

STEP 3: GUIDE

Depersonalize the situation and present alternative perspectives: Around
the age of seven or eight, children are better able to take others'

perspectives into account. Knowing this, you can help your daughter depersonalize what she has likely experienced as an "attack" from her best friends. For example, here, Mom or Dad could have helped Fiona understand that the pressure from her friends was not about *her*, or how much they liked (or didn't like) her. Rather, it was about *them* and their need to solidify their belonging to the group. Girls often feel stronger as part of a group, and thus, they don't want to be the only ones doing something "risky" or sharing something about themselves that makes them feel vulnerable. If everyone participates, each girl is taking "equal risk."

The pressure they put on Fiona was not to make her unhappy, although it obviously had that result. Instead, it was to stop *themselves* from feeling vulnerable and alone. Understanding this will not take away the pain that Fiona felt, but it can help mitigate the possible long-term effects it could have on her sense of self, or her feelings about her "place" in the group.

Help your child understand her own friendship group: Parents have an important role to play in guiding girls to observe and evaluate for *themselves* the importance of groups in general, and their specific group at the moment. For example, ask your daughter who usually has the final say in group decisions. See if you can connect with her about how she feels about her ability to share her ideas or what she does when she disagrees with a group decision. Is she close friends with all members, or just one or two? By supporting your child in developing a framework of understanding about her own group, you give her the necessary tools to choose whether she wants to stay part of a group while staying true to herself, or reevaluate her participation on a larger level.

Dialogue about power imbalances and bullying: Many girls allow social power plays to continue or escalate because they see them as different from "real" bully issues. Additionally, girls often feel these conflicts are not "bad enough" to warrant parental guidance. Similarly, they may have trouble seeing one of their good friends as a bully. It is useful to talk with your daughter about the fact that children can *act* in bullying ways without necessarily *being* bullies all of the time. See appendix 1 for examples of more subtle forms of bullying. This perspective will enable you and your child to look at hurtful situations in more supportive and productive ways. When you help her understand the *impact of actions* (as opposed to focusing on whether or not they should be labeled "bullying"), you open the door to connecting, guiding, and supporting her to act in new and more powerful ways.

Here, Mom could have said, "Wow, Fiona, you did a really great job knowing what you were comfortable playing and what you weren't. You seem upset about how things went. The feeling you have inside isn't your fault. Sometimes our friends' decisions can leave us feeling really bad. That doesn't mean they can't still be our friends. But it does mean we have to know what is *our* problem and what is *their* problem, and this really is *their* problem. I'm so glad you told me about it so I can help you feel better about what happened and realize what a wonderful job you did sticking up for yourself!"

Tips for Girls: The Difference Between Gossiping
and Checking-In

There is a difference between gossiping with your friends about a classmate, and checking in with a trusted adult about a concern you have for a peer. In this book, we emphasize how important it is to keep private information private. However, a secret should make you smile, and it should not be a burden to keep. If there's ever a time when your friend's secret makes you uneasy in any way, you should approach a trusted adult about it. Listen to your instincts and trust yourself! You should always have support around any information—secret or not—that is making you uneasy.

STEP 4: SUPPORT TO ACT

Give her some (more) personal power: In the heat of the moment, it's difficult for girls to think of things to say that leave them feeling powerful. Some ideas:

❖ *Have her say it to herself:* Often it can be hard to feel good about yourself when things with friends are rocky. Suggest some positive phrases your daughter can practice saying in her head about herself *while she is at home*, where they can be memorized. Practicing in front of a mirror might help (see "Mirror, Mirror" box). This will make it easier to draw on them when she is stressed or down. For instance:

- ✿ "I am fun to be with and lots of kids like being my friend."
- ✿ "I like playing alone—I can think up fun adventures!"
- ✿ "Being alone gives me a chance to think."
- ✿ "My games are fun to play, even if that is not what my friends want to play right now."
- ✿ "I can decide to rejoin my friends when I am ready."
- ✿ "I am proud of myself for staying true to ME!"

Have her say it out loud: Help your daughter know that just because her friends think or say something does not mean she has to agree. So have her practice saying these one-liners aloud at home or away from friends and then try out some at school:

- ✿ "Friends don't always agree, and that's okay."
- ✿ "I think I'll just watch this round."
- ✿ "You all go ahead, I'm fine."
- ✿ "That's your opinion."
- ✿ "I can play the game this way."

You will want to help your daughter assert herself in an emotion-free way, as opposed to using a tone of voice that conveys frustration or that she is trying to convince someone of something (see "Assert Yourself," on page 88, for more).

- ✿ ***Silent strength:*** Make necklaces or pins with your daughter that you can *both* wear, affix to a backpack/

Tips for Girls: Mirror, Mirror

When practicing saying positive phrases about yourself in front of the mirror, think about your:

- Gaze (looking down seems passive; rolling your eyes is aggressive; looking straight ahead is assertive)
- Shoulder position (shoulders hunched seems passive; shoulders back is assertive)
- Facial expression (scared seems passive; angry seems aggressive; friendly is assertive)
- Voice (wavering seems passive; loud or angry seems aggressive; strong, kind, and even is assertive)
- Body position (shuffling feet or swaying body seems passive; leaning forward seems aggressive; standing tall with feet firmly planted is assertive)

TEACHER'S Tip: Charades and Reader's Theater

A playful way to help all your students develop a better understanding of how to use their bodies to effectively communicate is charades. To do this, give out two cards, each with an emotion written on it. Each child gets a turn to use her body (no words) to convey two different emotions: "angry" versus "sad," etc. Stick with simple emotions for younger children, but, with practice, most can begin to recognize "scared" versus "shy" versus "bossy" and so on. It's a great vocabulary enhancer as well!

If you are looking for a more "academic" way to introduce these issues, think about Reader's Theater! Talk to the children about "body lines," where a character conveys emotion or action through only his or her body (for example, the troll looks grumpy or the queen is puzzled). Connect this to everyday life by commenting to your students about how we often don't realize we are "talking," but not with our mouths! Have students practice "body lines" as they read (and reread!) their play . . . you will often find even shy students are more comfortable trying out assertive postures in this context.

purse, or carry in your pocket. When your daughter is feeling stressed, outnumbered, or ganged up on, have her clench it in her hands or rub her fingers over it, to remind her of the team of support she has outside her friendship group. Let your daughter see how you gain strength and comfort from this reminder of *her* when you're stuck in traffic or having a bad day.

✤ *Suggest that she try to shape the play:* According to Dr. Thompson, nine-year-olds begin to covet material possessions, and experience with them increases social standing. For example, in times of awkward group dynamics, your daughter can bring out an object, such as a trendy toy or jump rope. She can also attempt to redirect the play by reverting to an accepted fantasy, such as playing a group-invented game of Lava Monster. She can similarly invite a change in context by suggesting hopscotch, four square, or swings.

Help her form individual friendships with group members: In order for your daughter's suggestions to have traction, she will need at least one ally in the group to back her idea. This is when being a fringe member of the group is a big disadvantage. One way to solidify friendships is by cultivating relationships outside the group environment. When girls make individual connections and bring these connections back to the group, they have a stronger presence within it. Thus, they are less likely to be pushed when tested, and when they are pushed, they will have additional support to withstand it or redirect it.

TEACHER'S Tip: Partnering Girls

Pair girls attempting to make one-on-one connections as reading buddies or math partners to help lay the foundation for social connections outside of class, such as during recess.

When the Group Turns Against Your Child

This story highlights the struggle girls go through when their group turns on them and they need to start over. The suggestions apply to scenarios where girls are ousted (or threatened to be ousted) by their friendship circle.

Letting go of a friendship circle

Since the beginning of fifth grade, Reyna's daughter Natasha and Maddie had been best friends. In addition to playdates, they spent virtually every recess together, along with Jaden, Kelsie, and Livy. Midyear, they began learning how to play Chinese jump rope. Maddie was very coordinated, and her skill made her the group jumping leader; she organized the way the girls rotated in and out of being enders (rope holders) and so forth. One day she announced there would be tryouts for their Chinese jump rope "team." The group would have a few weeks to practice, but any girl who was not able to do the twenty jumps in the routine that Maddie and Jaden (the other strong personality in the group) decided on would be kicked off the team.

Natasha felt this expectation was unfair, and after problem solving with Reyna about ways to approach her friends, Natasha told Maddie that teamwork and being a good sport should be what makes a team, not how many jumps someone might do correctly. While Maddie agreed with Natasha that sportsmanship was part of being on a team, she also believed strongly that executing the routine skillfully was key. With the date of Maddie's imposed tryouts drawing near, the group began to split. Jaden and Maddie—the two strongest jumpers and the two strongest personalities—lobbied hard to move forward with the tryouts. Kelsie and Livy at first were unsure how they felt about possibly losing their friendship group if they could not do the difficult routine. However, wanting to align with who they saw as the more powerful players, both went along (somewhat reluctantly) with Jaden and Maddie, making it a four-against-one situation.

One day at recess, Maddie was absent. Jaden complained to Natasha about how the group dynamic had changed, and Natasha reiterated her concerns about cutting girls from the team. "Don't you think this is crazy?" Natasha asked Jaden. "I wish Maddie weren't being so bossy about the tryouts. Can't we just go back to having fun jumping?" When Jaden reported to Maddie what Natasha had said, Maddie took Natasha's comment as evidence that Natasha had betrayed their friendship. An irreparable rift ensued. While the girls were not openly cruel to Natasha, they began excluding her from their after-school get-togethers. She continued to hang out with them at recess, but they made no bones about laughing about the fun they had had at their weekend events (to which she had not been invited). They often walked by her without talking to her, or started games without asking her to join. Natasha's self-confidence began to falter, and she started to dread going to school.

What happened and why?

Like many girls, Natasha found herself on the wrong end of a group freeze-out. As is common in such forms of exclusion, the more powerful girls (Maddie and Jaden) closed rank around the less powerful followers (Livy and Kelsie) to purposefully leave Natasha out of the group. They then tightened the bonds between them by creating new group memories through shared experiences that Natasha was actively excluded from; in doing so, they solidified their new identity as a group without her. Talking about these shared experiences in front of Natasha was a way of helping them to feel "in" (and more like a group) *because* Natasha was being left "out."

As is also common, one girl in the group begins the "taking sides" dynamic in an attempt to assert her power, or to better align herself with another girl in the group. In this case, Jaden sided with Maddie's desire to do the tryouts, creating a "power block" in the group. With her position firm, Jaden then worked to get the other girls to side against Natasha's more inclusive jump rope policy. Not surprisingly, it was Jaden who put the nail in the coffin for Natasha by getting Natasha to open up to her when they were alone, only to then report select (and incriminating) items back to Maddie. In this way, you can see how one powerful girl, in a surprisingly short period of time, is able to manipulate an entire group and influence longstanding friendships in devastating ways.

What Natasha did well

She stood up for what she believed to be just: Kudos to Natasha for being willing to state her beliefs and stand by them, despite being a lonely voice among her peers. In so doing, she gave her group the chance to address conflict openly, without the "behind-the-back" discussions that often break apart friendship circles. Unfortunately (but not unexpectedly), the group did not alter its position. While the outcome left Natasha devastated, her ability to identify her values, articulate them, and stand by them is admirable.

She stood by her group for as long as possible: As we have discussed previously, all children want and need to be part of the social scene at school. And all social groups will struggle at various points along the way. Giving up a friendship or a friendship circle at the first sign of trouble leaves girls socially isolated. In order for friendships to grow, they will, at some point, face conflict. Those friendships that survive are stronger as a result.

Applying the Four Steps: Strategies to use with your own daughter

STEPS 1 & 2: OBSERVE AND CONNECT

Foresight is 20/20: Reyna had been hearing about the wonderful aspects of Maddie and Natasha's friendship for many months. She knew the other players and personalities in the group as well, from discussions with Natasha and her own interactions with the girls. When Natasha began to describe some of the group conflict, she and Reyna could quickly connect over how that made her daughter feel, what she thought was fair, and so on.

And as proud as Reyna was of Natasha's belief in and public assertion about allowing all participating members to stay on the team, she was also able to foresee that the conflict was likely to cause division within the group. Especially because of *which* girls were on the two sides of the issue. If one of the less powerful girls like Kelsie had been the one pushing for the tryouts, Maddie might have backed Natasha's position, even if she herself had felt more on-the-fence. With an additional ally in Natasha's corner, the likelihood of Jaden's being able to divide the group would have been greatly diminished, because there would not have been one powerful block (Maddie and Jaden) that could sway the other members so completely.

However, with no additional girl to stand up to Maddie and Jaden (or to side with Natasha), the group dynamic shifted and Natasha's lone position became a threat to the solidarity the other girls were trying to establish. Because Reyna knew this group so well, she was able to observe what was unfolding, and thus could connect with and guide Natasha from relatively early on. In your own home, listening to your daughter's social stories in good times and getting to know her friends will allow you to more

---

TEACHER'S Tip: Cliques vs. Groups

Sometimes teachers see the writing on the wall before their students can. If you notice rising tension between pairs of girls or within friendship circles, use your positive influence to provide social options—or social breaks—for group members. Think about changing the room configuration, mixing up partner pairs, asking two potentially well-matched girls to help you sort papers at recess, and so on.

It can make all the difference when teachers notice when a *group* turns into a *clique*. Some ways to spot the shift:

CLIQUE	GROUP
• Uses behaviors that *inhibit* teaching/learning	• Uses behaviors that *support* teaching/learning
• Expects uniformity, homogeneity	• Builds on individual positive qualities
• Works at excluding and being exclusive	• Works at including and being inclusive
• Has a dictatorial leader	• Has leaders that *emerge naturally* because of positive attributes

As we mentioned earlier, if social groupings interfere with teaching, learning, or sustaining your Caring Community, you have a role and right to guide and support your students to act.

quickly and skillfully help her navigate group dynamics as friendships shift and change.

STEP 3: GUIDE

Help your child understand the group dynamic: As we have described previously, one goal of the Four Steps is to help your child depersonalize social struggles. This is no easy task, especially when strong emotions are involved. However, when girls understand that what is happening to them is not only common, but even expected—not because of *them* but because of *how groups at this stage of development work*—it can help them separate out feelings of blame or guilt from feelings of sadness or loss. Being able to better identify these emotions will help her to process the situation effectively, remain more confident, and begin to make more powerful choices.

For Natasha this meant understanding who had the power, and how it was used to isolate her. Reyna was able to help Natasha see how Jaden manipulated the situation: sidling up to Maddie, creating a power block, turning the group against her, warming herself to Natasha to get her to open up, reporting back to Maddie exactly the right thing to tip the scales in her favor, and so on. It is amazing how sneaky some girls can be, even at these young ages! While Natasha certainly was a player in the drama, many of the parts were cast in a way that was beyond her control. Knowing this gave Natasha new perspective, a better ability to judge character moving forward, and a sense of where she stood in terms of making active choices.

Some girls appear to come pre-wired to sense group dynamics

and power structures within friendship circles. Reyna's other daughter, Nadia, has displayed this quality from a very young age. Even as a kindergartener, she often made comments like, "When Katie and I try to play with Danielle and Erica, it never works. Danielle is so sassy! She always pulls Erica to where she wants and orders me and Katie around. It's no fun playing with them and every time I try, I think the same thing!" When asked why she continued to try, Nadia stated matter-of-factly, "Well, maybe one day Danielle will grow nicer or Erica will just tell her to leave her alone! Plus, it's no big deal. When Danielle starts getting sassy, I just grab Katie's hand and we go off to play chipmunks under the play structure without her."

This type of skill serves "tuned-in" girls well, although it is certainly no magic antidote to social cruelty and friendship struggles. Thus, use your guidance to *extend* the skill set she already has. All girls will face social strife, even girls like Nadia.

Help your child see her friend's perspective: Even if you know the friendship between your child and her best friend is over (or you want it to be!), helping your child see her friend's perspective is extremely valuable. Being sensitive to different points of view will help her in future social situations. In addition, if your child can see her friend's perspective—*not necessarily agree with her but better understand her point of view*—she can plan appropriate action without turning into a Mean Girl herself. As we stress throughout this book, no one is served if the fight keeps going, because what inevitably happens is that things escalate (see chapter 6 for what to do when your child acts like a Mean Girl).

In this situation, Reyna was able to help Natasha see that

Maddie felt so powerful in her new role as group leader that she was not capable of understanding how that position was possibly being used to the detriment of the other girls. From Maddie's perspective, the tryouts were evidence of group commitment. Understanding this did not change what Natasha was feeling, but it made it less personal.

Identify the role of talking behind a friend's back: While it is normal and natural to want to "vent" about one friend to another, doing so will often get your child into trouble. As with e-mails or video clips, once disparaging words are out there, your child has absolutely no control over *if, when, how,* and *to whom* the words will be repeated or distorted. Your child also has no control over how other children (or the target child) will interpret the comments, because she may not be there when the words are relayed. Reyna helped Natasha see that even though Natasha didn't think she was saying anything particularly inflammatory (because the conflict was already out in the open), calling Maddie "bossy" was hurtful, and it led to the "final straw" in Maddie's mind.

Brainstorm a list of possible actions: Your child always has choices, but it probably doesn't feel this way to her, and this is why the Four-Step plan is so vital. While we cannot promise that the choices will be ideal, helping your child understand her social options and the support she will have from you as she acts on them will make all the difference in the world. There is nothing harder than watching your child struggle or feeling her disappointment and heartache, but when you work as a team to better understand her situation and help her to regain her power, you'll both be better equipped to move on. As we suggest in all social situations, together come up with a list of every imaginable choice your child has, and whittle down the list to those that are possible/feasible. And remember, as your child makes her decisions and things unfold, you may need to revisit and revise your options.

Sharing Stories: Many of us can feel Natasha's angst because we, too, have similar stories of friendships lost or betrayed. Reyna shared with Natasha how she had changed friend groups midway through middle school. She related how hard it was to lose close friends she had had for many years. Hearing how her own mom had faced these same issues made a tremendous impression on Natasha and gave her just the courage she needed to face the very hard choices she had to make.

STEP 4: SUPPORT TO ACT

Should I stay . . . ?: The most basic decision that a girl in this type of situation needs to make is if she wants to try to repair things with her friendship circle or if she needs to move on. As parents, you may have strong opinions one way or another, and there may come a time when you need to make your perspective understood in order to preserve your daughter's health and well-being. However, until that point, the goal is to use the Four Steps to observe, connect, guide, and support your daughter to act. Girls in situations like this often feel powerless. Thus, use Active Listening to really hear what your daughter feels and wants to try to do to empower herself. If she decides she wants to try to mend things with her friends, you can support her to:

- *Build relationships with individual group members outside of school*: The group dynamic was set and the lines were drawn. If Natasha wanted to try to change things, she would need to do some reintegrating by solidifying one-on-one relationships. Given the precarious nature of the situation, having structured and fun activities would likely have been necessary (going for ice cream, going ice-skating).

- *Make amends*: Even though Natasha did not mean to speak badly about Maddie "behind her back," she did tell Jaden she thought Maddie was being "bossy." If Natasha wanted to try to fix things with her friendship circle, she would need to approach Maddie separately and apologize to her. (For more on how to make amends, see "Reflections on Talking Badly About Your Friend" box.) Because the girls were such good friends, both mothers did actually take the girls out to eat to help them try and talk things through. Unfortunately, while discussions were civil and seemingly productive, Natasha continued to feel excluded at school. Reyna and Natasha knew they had to revisit the Four Steps and adjust their choices accordingly.

Tips for Girls: Reflections on Talking Badly
About Your Friend

Sometimes when we are frustrated or annoyed with one friend, it is hard not to say unkind things about her to another friend. If this has happened with you (we all have been there, so don't worry!) it may be worth doing some writing-thinking in your journal. Examine your feelings about why you wanted to pass on the rumor or speak against your friend. Write some about it. Was it:

- To get "in" with a group? (Next time you can talk about and make plans based on shared interests.)
- Because this person had done something annoying or hurtful to you? (Next time, try using "I statements." See page 91.)
- To make you feel powerful or knowledgeable? (Next time, think about ways to assert yourself and share your ideas. See "Assert Yourself!," on page 88).
- To show that you knew something personal or secretive that others did not know? (Next time, try to connect with a shared interest.)
- Because you were feeling jealous? (Next time, focus on things you have done that you're proud of.)
- Because you were you feeling bored? (Next time, suggest an activity!)
- Because you were you looking for solidarity and support from another by having her agree with you? (Next time, try talking about upsetting situations without naming a specific girl. So instead of saying, "Can you believe Sasha is such a drama queen? Don't you hate it when she exaggerates every little thing?" try, "Don't you hate drama queens? It drives me crazy when they make everything into a big deal." Even if

your confidante says, "I know. Sasha can be such a pain," keep it neutral with a reply such as, "Well, I know lots of girls who act like that! It's such a pain.")

- Because you felt pressured to share a secret to solidify your friendship with another girl? (To counter pressure you feel when a friend says, "Oh, you can trust me with Cindy's secret. If we were really good friends, you'd tell me," try saying, "It's important to me that all my friends know they can trust me. That means I never tell secrets, even to really great friends. And, now you know that I would never tell anyone else a secret that you might share with me!")

Knowing *why* you acted as you did, and thinking of some alternatives, will let you make different choices next time. If you regret having passed on the rumor or spoken behind your friend's back, what decisions can you make next time? What about right now?

Read about the Three Rs, on page 207, for more on how you might move forward when you realize you acted unkindly, or see "Tokens of Friendship," on page 228, for ways to approach your friend.

TEACHER'S Tip: Friendship Puppets

Sometimes, all a girl needs to feel ready to act is time to reflect on her own convictions. Have your students create construction paper puppets and have a discussion about how important it is to know what qualities they are looking for in a friend, and what kinds of things they should do to be a good friend. Students can then cut out or draw words or pictures on the puppets to reflect the attributes they are seeking in friends, or ways they show friendship to peers. Hang the "puppets" around the classroom.

. . . or should I go now?: Deciding to break away from a friendship group is a huge decision for a child. Until the pain of staying the same is greater than the pain of changing, children won't make a permanent change. But, when they are ready, you can help. Upon realizing that nothing would fix the friendship with Maddie because of continued exclusion from the group, Natasha made the excruciating decision to break away from her friendship circle in the spring. If your daughter finds herself making a similar decision, think about supporting her in the following ways:

- ✿ *Look for someone who needs a friend*: What happened to Natasha is not unique, so it is quite likely that there is another girl in your daughter's class or grade who is looking for a friend. Michelle remembers being new to her school in fourth grade. With all the groups already formed, it felt difficult to make friends. Until she met Helen, who had recently been ousted from her friendship circle. The two connected and have been best friends ever since. Support your child to think about who in her class (or in another class) might be someone open to new friendship because she is new or newly "unattached."

- ✿ *Strengthen out-of-school friends*: Your child spends most of her day at school, and having friends there is vital to her sense of well-being. However, when things are precarious for her at school, fortifying friendships outside of school can build her confidence. Think of some family friends, cousins, and friends from after-school activities whom your child can connect with as she finds her way to new friendships at school.

❧ *Get more involved in after-school activities:* While you don't want to overcommit your child, if there is a period of time when playdates dwindle or invitations to parties disappear, see if she is interested in exploring another skill, talent, or ability outside of school.

❧ *Connect with another friendship group:* It may be that by midyear, all the girls have friendship groups, or that the ones who don't are simply not a match for your child. In this case, she may need to try to get to know a new group of girls. Just have your daughter be sure this new group does not overlap with the group she is trying to move away from! One effective way to approach a new group is if your child focuses on an individual within the group—one girl whom she feels she can try and befriend. It is often easiest if this girl is in your daughter's class. Rather than trying to pull this new friend away from her group, the goal is for the new friend to help ease your daughter's transition into the *already established group.*

Natasha chose to do just that. One day at lunch she smiled politely at Maddie and the others, but sat down to eat beside Stella. She made a point to ask Stella if she could play with her group at recess. The next day, Natasha looked for Stella as the class made their way to the lunchroom, and walked near her. She waited for Stella near the hot lunch exit and then sat with Stella at her table again, after which she asked again if she could play with her and her friends at recess. Stella said it was fine, but did ask, "Why are you not playing with Maddie anymore? I thought you guys were best friends." Keeping her composure, and not wanting to throw oil on the fire of what was already a tense situation, Natasha replied, "It's just that Maddie seems to want to play with only Jaden right now." In this way, Natasha was honest but neither mean nor blaming.

If going up to a new child at school seems too hard for your child at first, set up an out-of-school playdate to help develop the friendship.

Avoid becoming a Mean Girl: It's natural that your daughter would be hurt and angry about what is happening to her. Knowing this, she will need your support to make healthy choices that help her to grow and/or move on without becoming a Mean Girl herself. Getting involved in spreading rumors or gossip may make her feel better in the short run, but will be a disservice to her in the long run. Thus, when breaking away, you may need to role-play with your child about how to be friendly without needing to be "friends." Remember, no one benefits if the fight continues. Help your daughter to let go without fanning the flames of anger or misery. For example, Reyna encouraged Natasha to talk to Maddie when Maddie initiated a conversation but to not seek Maddie out. She also suggested that Natasha continue to smile at Maddie politely and assertively, rather than glare at her aggressively or look away passively.

Celebrate small successes: Being de-friended or ousted from a friendship group is never easy. To begin to move forward and make new choices takes a tremendous amount of courage, so be sure your child knows how proud you are of her—and how proud she should be of herself! Help her recognize small victories, and celebrate small successes. These may be as simple as commenting on your daughter making a phone call for a playdate with a new friend, or a morning that your child wakes up without feeling nervous about running into her old friends. Natasha, for example, experienced her first small success upon her return from a Memorial Day weekend trip. Waiting for her in the mail was an invitation to the birthday party of one of the girls in Stella's circle—a tangible sign that she had indeed become an accepted and included member in this new group of girls!

6

All Girls Can Be Mean: When Your Daughter Is Acting Like a Mean Girl

"Sugar and spice and everything nice . . . that's what little girls are made of." And while of course you know this rhyme is not all true, you are equally aware that there are a great many cultural pressures on girls to be "good," "sweet," and "nice" (that is, passive). Interestingly, there are also a great many cultural pressures to *not* be so good, sweet, and nice—to instead be tough, firm, and determined (aggressive). With all these different messages and pressures, what is a girl to do?

The goal is to help your daughter find a way to be both kind and tough at the same time—to be *assertive*. Being assertive means being sweet and considerate *mixed with* being tough and determined. Finding this balance is no easy task, and most girls will flip-flop from passive (too nice) to aggressive (too mean) while trying to hit the mark on assertiveness. Even adults struggle along these same lines!

It is for this reason that we make the distinction between a girl "*acting* like a bully" and a girl "*being* a bully." Make no mistake, there are girl bullies out there. If your child is one of them, we suggest you utilize this book to its fullest. But you may also find you need additional professional support that goes beyond the scope of this book. However, more often than not, you are likely to find that much of the Mean Girl behavior is done by girls who are various degrees of "good" and "nice." They are simply trying to fit in and belong, and making mistakes along the way as they search for that creative balance called assertiveness. Unfortunately, by (ineffectively) trying to find their place in their group or with their friends, or (unsuccessfully) attempting to stand up for themselves, they can inadvertently cross the line to aggressiveness or meanness and hurt those they care about.

If you find yourself concerned that your daughter is acting meanly, follow the Four-Step process. Once you see where her actions are coming from, you can support her in making new, more balanced choices. In this chapter, we take a look at what happens when nice girls act mean, and what parents and other supportive adults can do to change the dynamic.

There Are Two Sides to Every Story

This story highlights the struggles children go through when they try (ineffectively) to assert themselves with their friends. The suggestions apply to scenarios where children act meanly while attempting to get their needs met.

Ellie's Side

Hailey had been Ellie's best friend for as long as she could remember. But in first grade, Ellie felt like Hailey was "different." "All of the sudden, everything needs to be *her* way," Ellie explained to us. "Like she's the queen or something. There she is, telling all of us what part we are in the game, making all the rules. It just got to be no fun being around her.

"Then she asked me to do the talent show with her. I thought, *here's where I can be the leader!* I told her my idea about playing piano together. She said no to that right away. The only thing she wanted to do was a handstand routine, and she *knows* I don't like gymnastics. When I brought up maybe doing a dance instead, she just said, 'No way!' I was like, 'Fine,' but when I talked to my dad about it, he told me that I needed to stand up for myself. He said I needed to have more than just her as a friend. I really like Hailey when she isn't being so bossy. I didn't want to hurt her feelings. So I just told her I didn't want to do the talent show anymore.

"But she wouldn't let it go. She kept following me around asking me about it, telling me she didn't want to make me do the show if I didn't want to. So I finally just told her—I *did* want to do the show, just not with her! My new friend Zunera liked *all* my ideas. We decided to play piano together for the show, just like I'd wanted to do with Hailey before she got all bossy about it."

What happened and why?

Ellie did not wake up one day and decide to be cruel to her best friend. She actually had spent too long trying to be *nice*. For too long she bottled up her annoyance when Hailey controlled their play. With Ellie's father's suggestion to stand up for herself (but with little guidance and no plan on how to follow through), she chose an ineffective means of doing so. That is, she didn't deal with the ongoing situation or her friend directly. Instead, she avoided the true issue and backed out of the dynamic by saying she didn't want to do the show, when in fact she did. This indirect means of dealing with confrontation is common in both children and adults . . . unless there is a plan in place to give girls the connection, the guidance, and the support to act in more effective ways.

Just as common is the newfound power that children such as Hailey feel in their close friendships. Close friendships provide girls with a forum to begin experimenting with new ways of interacting. These new ways include asserting their control, often ineffectively—not with the express purpose of being bossy, mean, or hurtful, but rather to begin to learn how to influence play in increasingly powerful ways. It is no surprise then that Hailey (who also had no guidance or plan for how to be assertive rather than bossy) attempted to wield her power in ineffective and inadvertently unkind ways.

What Ellie did well

She sought support: When Ellie neared her breaking point, she reached out to her dad for help. How lucky for both of them that Ellie felt she could go to him in a time of need. In hearing his daughter's angst, Dad took the opportunity to instill a valuable message—don't let your friend walk all over you. Unfortunately, like most well-meaning parents who do not have the framework of the Four Steps to draw on, his directive was not matched with an assertive, child-directed plan.

She tried to stand up for herself within the friendship: Ellie had, for too long, allowed the balance of power in the friendship to tip so that Hailey had (and expected) too much control. This commonly occurs in even the very best of friendships for periods of time. If efforts are not made by one or both girls to rectify things, one girl often feeds off the power she has, while the other silently seethes until a breaking point is reached. Neither condition is in either girl's best interests. To her credit, Ellie recognized that something in her friendship with Hailey needed to change.

She took her friend's feelings into account: Contrary to what we may have thought when we read Hailey's side of the story (see page 93), Ellie is in fact a very nice girl. Even with her dad's directive to have more of a spine, she thought about Hailey and did not want to hurt her wonderful friend, regardless of the fact that Hailey had been too bossy lately. As Michelle's children would say, "Hippos for Ellie!" However, because it often takes so much for nice girls to assert their needs, their attempts often come out as over-the-top demands. Thus, it is exactly *because* Ellie is so nice that, in trying to move from being passive to assertive, she slipped into being aggressive. Here is where the Four-Step plan can help!

Applying the Four Steps: Strategies to use with your own daughter

You might feel that Ellie's actions were somewhat justified—that she was not in fact that "mean," given how Hailey had been acting previously. However, remember that the goal of the Four Steps is to give your child the tools and skills to more effectively manage social situations. Girls' relationships will often seesaw back and forth in terms of who has the power. And mean acts tend to escalate, as opposed to resolve, issues. As parents, you want to help your child solve her problems without throwing oil on the fire of an already volatile social situation. Thus, there is a tremendous amount your child can learn from the Four Steps about asserting herself in kind and respectful ways.

STEP 1: OBSERVE

There's a lot to notice and talk about: Even with a straightforward issue such as this, there is a lot Ellie's dad could have noticed and thought about. Having a more comprehensive view of the situation would have helped him to find the best means to connect, and the most appropriate ways to guide and support Ellie to act. For example:

- ✿ Actively Listening to how Ellie felt to have all her talent show ideas rejected, as well as the larger friendship struggles she and Hailey were having
- ✿ Finding out more about the active role Ellie *had* played in the friendship up to this point, even if these were

small or ineffective attempts to assert herself or regain power in the relationship

❖ Noticing how Ellie interacts in her other relationships. Is she continuously passive, or is there something different about this friendship? Is this passivity a change, or has it been consistent for a while?

❖ Thinking about other aspects of her life—changes in a family situation, failure on another front (losing out on an audition, poor performance on a test), the ending to a school year, or other life factors that might be playing into this situation.

❖ Noticing what happened between when Ellie said she didn't want to do the show and when the meanness escalated to the "I want to do it but not with you" assertion.

STEP 2: CONNECT

Celebrate the connection you have . . . : It is evident that Dad and Ellie have a strong connection and she feels she can go to him when times get tough. If you have a similar relationship with your child, tell her how happy you are that she came to you, and how much you appreciate the opportunity to work together as a team to face these difficult issues together. Continue to develop this relationship outside of moments of crisis, taking advantage of the activities suggested in the "Think, Share, Do . . ." chapters. If you feel you and your daughter do not (yet) share this kind of bond, begin forging it with the activities in the "Think, Share, Do . . ." chapters.

. . . but make it stronger: As much as Ellie trusts her dad and his opinion, she only initiated an interaction with him when she felt like things were "bad enough." One goal we have is to help your child learn she can come to you with the "little stuff" long before it turns into "big stuff," and that (as much as possible) *you will give equal attention to both!*

For example, if Ellie had spoken to her dad about her frustrations earlier, before the conflict escalated, he would have had the opportunity to guide Ellie more effectively. Remember, even if your child does not come to you directly, you can observe her at-home behaviors and listen to the friendship stories she shares to help you realize when there may be a door open for *you* to initiate a discussion regarding issues she may be dealing with.

STEP 3: GUIDE

As it stands now, Ellie may not feel like she needs any more guidance. In her mind, she stood up to her bossy friend, just like her dad told her to. She found a new friend who was ready to listen to her ideas about the talent show. However, despite the fact that Ellie feels like she is on easy street, there is still a great deal Ellie's dad could do to guide her, moving forward and looking back.

Get Playful: Don't forget the power of play in the lives of young children. Up until (and for some girls, even through) the teen years, girls benefit from hands-on fantasy play with dolls, puppets, etc. Instead of giving her yet another lecture or long-winded response on how to handle a situation, approach her in a playful way. As Dr. Larry Cohen, author of *Playful Parenting*, suggests, begin some of your interactions with "Let's pretend." Grab some Beanie Babies and say, "Let's pretend I'm Hailey and you're Ellie." Or, "Let's pretend I'm Ellie and you're Hailey." See where your daughter takes the interaction. Will she be able to release some latent anger? Great! Or try out different ways of asserting herself within the friendship? Also great! In fact, there is almost no

---

TEACHER'S Tip: Bursting Through Stressors

There are many playful ways to help girls better realize when they are reaching the breaking point, and what to do when that happens! For example, form a circle with one child in the center. When another child blows bubbles at her, have her pop the bubbles. Explain that sometimes stressors are like bubbles: they come at you, but if you have strategies and resources, you can deal with them (that is, pop them). Ask your students to talk about some stressors they deal with (schoolwork, friend fights), and some ways they deal with them. Now have *many* children blow bubbles at the child in the center. When the bubble barrage comes from all directions, it is harder to keep up with popping all of the bubbles. Explain that when there are too many stressors, children can feel overwhelmed and defeated—too many problems coming at you from too many directions are too overwhelming for one person to solve (pop) by herself.

So what can you do? You can ask for help! Have the child in the center ask a classmate or two to come into the middle with her to see how many more bubbles they can pop as a team. Ask them, aside from friends, who else is on their team? (Parents, teachers, other relatives, coaches, and so forth.)

---

wrong way for this scenario to unfold. So rather than try to direct the interaction too much, see where this lighthearted and impromptu role-playing will take you. If you don't get your message into the scenario today, remember, you can always play more tomorrow! Of course, if she gets angry and does role-playing in a way that worries you, use what you learn as an entry into applying the Four Steps to this new information, seeking additional help if necessary.

Stand up early and often: Too many girls, in an attempt to be nice (or because they feel underconfident), wait too long to begin asserting themselves in their interactions. Ellie is a case in point. For too long she sat by and got more and more annoyed about how Hailey was treating her, but she did little along the way to attempt to stand up for herself, assert appropriate power, and realign the amount of control she felt in the friendship. This is not Ellie's fault—as is true for most girls, no one had ever taught her how to act assertively! Here Ellie's dad could have helped her be more assertive along the way. Even if Ellie had felt she needed to break away from Hailey, she could have been supported to do so in a less aggressive, "not Mean Girl" way.

Two for the price of one: One thing that is magical about the Four Steps is how the assertive actions of one friend can positively influence the other. That is, if Ellie had approached the situation differently (been assertive in the face of Hailey's "bossiness," rather than alternatively passive and then aggressive), it would have provided the opportunity for *Hailey* to rectify the situation. When one girl asserts herself (appropriately), it gives the other girl the opportunity to reflect on her actions, and to make new, more balanced and considerate choices. In this way, one girl's assertiveness can influence another, or can change the dynamic of a situation so immensely that *both* girls benefit.

Thus, guiding in this situation is realizing that the goal is *not* to convince Ellie that Hailey is a bully and that therefore Ellie needs to stand up to her. Instead, the goal is to help Ellie see that *both girls* are finding their way and need support. Reread Hailey's version of the story (see page 93). Naturally, with the information available, everything in the Four Steps there was directed at helping Hailey to move forward in accepting and dealing with Ellie's rejection. Knowing Ellie's side of the story, we can now see Mom's missed opportunity to guide Hailey. Within the Four Steps, Hailey's mom could have supported her to make different choices when controlling the situation regarding the talent show (and other areas of play). Hailey's mom could have also supported her daughter to repair the friendship by drawing on the three Rs.

The three Rs: When girls act meanly, it is beneficial for them to go through a process of identifying their actions and the ramifications:

- ✧ **Recognize** the mistake: Help your child identify the mistake she made, or that she hurt someone. If your child has trouble doing this, see "Feeling it in her core" (page 202) for some ideas.
- ✧ Be **Responsible**: Help your child avoid denying what she did, making an excuse for it, or blaming another person

(even if it happened as a result of another's actions, or if she felt pressured by someone else to act in a mean way). Part of making amends is owning her part of what happened, even if others have yet to own theirs. Your daughter has the power to stop the cycle with your help.

❖ **Rectify** what she can: Have her apologize, listen to her friend's feelings, and make an extra effort to show how she has changed or is doing things differently. Encourage an "I statement": "I'm sorry about ___. I think this happened because ___. Next time I will___. How are you feeling now?" (For more on "I Statements," see page 91.)

Both Ellie and Hailey could have taken advantage of the three Rs. However, be aware that if your child is in a situation like this one—where both girls acted in a way that was hurtful to the other—you may find that your child's friend does not recognize her role, accept responsibility, or try to rectify the situation. This may be because she does not realize the part she played, because she does not have the benefit of the Four-Step plan to help her, or because she continues to feel it is not her problem. While this can make things more difficult for your child, or more disappointing, it will not change the importance of her identifying and working through *her* role in the situation.

Note that helping your child own her part of the conflict is *not* intended to make the situation "her fault" (be sure to tell her this). The goal is *not* to get her to accept undue responsibility, nor to do all the work to try and fix the friendship. Instead, it is to give her support in identifying her own actions (and reactions), her behaviors, and her own solutions, which may include recognizing the limitation of a given friendship. One sign of a self-confident and caring person, at any age, is her ability to work through the three Rs. How lucky your daughter is that you are helping her learn this valuable skill!

TEACHER'S Tip: Filling a Bucket with Kindness

When you see dynamics such as this in your classroom, think about taking advantage of the Four-Step process and see what bringing the girls together (where appropriate) and really listening to each other (with your guidance and support) can uncover.

You can also encourage your Caring Community by making a special effort to notice and encourage kindness in your classroom every day:

- During a class meeting, have your students complement others on kind acts they witnessed that day or have a Class Kindness journal they can write in anonymously (with you then sharing the entries with the group).
- Unify the children around the goal of kindness by asking them to do kind things for their reading buddies, make thank-you cards for the school nurse, and so on.
- Read *Have You Filled a Bucket Today?* by Carol McCloud. Create an interactive bulletin board display where each child has a bucket. Invite students to write kind words or actions they have done for one another and literally fill each other's buckets. Keep an eye out for less full buckets to encourage your Caring Community to step up and appreciate each classmate!

Tips for Girls: Carry on the Kindness

Sometimes we don't act as kindly as we would like. But we are always in control of our choices to be kind moving forward. Think of three random acts of kindness to do, just because. Don't call public attention to yourself, just do them to spread a feeling of good cheer! Some ideas:

- Smile at 5 people.
- Thank the bus driver as you leave.
- Sit next to a girl who usually sits alone.
- Introduce yourself to the new child in class.
- Help your younger sister with her homework.
- Read a book to your younger brother.
- Invite a new friend into your games at recess.
- Hug your sibling, friend, and parent(s).
- Compliment at least three people.
- Hold the door for the person behind you.
- Say thank-you five times.
- Notice someone's hard work and comment on it to them.
- Offer to help someone.
- Make a card or some cookies for someone.
- Ask your parents to read you *Have You Filled a Bucket Today?* by Carol McCloud. Think of five ways you can fill someone's bucket today!

Don't forget—these small acts of kindness are a great way to Rectify if you have hurt a friend—think of some of your own to add to the list!

STEP 4: SUPPORT TO ACT

Girl get-togethers: While this solution is not appropriate in all situations, helping your child deal with her friend directly, with each girl having an advocate present, can be immensely beneficial. Both girls need to be willing to do this, along with both parents. In addition, it is often helpful if the parents have spoken separately beforehand, so they feel they know each girl's side of the story before walking in to the get-together. You may also want to do some role-playing with your child beforehand, to help her feel like she can express herself effectively. The more she practices this in low-stakes situations (with you or a helpful sibling), the more confidently she will approach her friend. Be mindful that even if you think you have a sense of how the conversation may go based on your interaction with the other child's parents, nobody controls another's actions. Therefore, there is no way to know for certain how the other girl will interact with your child in this moment.

Help the girls explain to one another how they've been feeling. The goal is to encourage each girl to speak, and to be heard and respected by the other (think of "I Statements" and the "Three Rs"). While it would be nice to reach new a understanding or to repair the friendship, this may not be possible. However, helping your child feel the power of speaking her mind in a kind and assertive way with you there to guide and support her is an invaluable experience, even if it does not salvage the immediate relationship.

Welcome a new friend: As we have said any number of times, having more than one good friend is a social safety net for your child. So in thinking about Hailey and Ellie's friendship, don't lose sight of the gift of the new friendship with girls like Zunera. Encourage your child as she reaches out to a new friend, and support her to act using her new assertiveness skills within that relationship!

Saying sorry: It happens to everyone—we reach a breaking point or act too quickly and wind up saying or doing something we wish we hadn't. Part of moving away from being a Mean Girl is working through the three Rs and going back and making amends for actions we regret. This is challenging even for adults! So work together with your child and support her as she figures out what she may want to do to Rectify the situation and apologize to her friend (see "Tokens of friendship," on page 228).

Remember, part of Ellie's apology would include honoring *why she acted as she did*. For example, she could say something like, "Hailey, I really like being your friend. But I was feeling like you weren't listening to my ideas and that what mattered to me didn't matter to you. I got really mad about it and I said some things that were mean and I'm sorry about that. I really just wanted to find a way to tell you the things I have been feeling for a while now."

Girls of any age can learn how to give heartfelt apologies. In this case, six-year-old Maya writes a spontaneous letter of apology to her sister after an argument. The letter reads, "Dear Kylie, I hope you are willing to talk to me. All I wanted to say is that I am really sorry if I felt mean to you. If you don't like my talk, please wait until I finish my sentence. Then you can tell me what you don't like in my sentences, and I will try my best to fix it. Believe me, times will be much better if you do that. Love, Maya."

The Power Rush of Popularity

This story highlights the struggles children go through when they get caught up in the wonderful feeling of being powerful within their group. The suggestions apply to scenarios where children act meanly because of the rush of excitement they get from being a group leader or an included member of a group.

Aliya's ascent

Aliya was a quiet, nice, smart girl who, as her mother had put it, "had the voice of an angel." She sang in a prestigious children's chorale, which had left her outside the social scene at her old school. Her friends saw her as an overachiever and were jealous of the ease of her "success." Her family moved just before third grade, to an arts-integrated magnet school. At the beginning of the year, Ronni had befriended her. The two were inseparable, and Aliya delighted in the best friendship they shared.

Things changed in January when Aliya won the lead role in the school play *Annie,* beating out even some fifth graders for the part. Suddenly, lots of girls were interested in hanging out with her and being her friend. She was included in many different playground games and group projects, and Ronni naturally went along. In no time, Aliya was the group leader and she felt powerful in a whole new way. She wished her family had switched schools years ago!

In late March, a few weeks before the big show, Aliya planned her birthday party. "I'm not sure I should invite Ronni to my slumber party," Aliya told her mother casually. "I'm not sure she really fits in with Sarah, Jessica, and Amanda." "Ronni has been a good friend to you since we moved here," her mother reminded her. "It would be very unkind to exclude her." Aliya reluctantly agreed.

At the party, the girls decided to give themselves manicures. "Here, Ronni," Sarah said, handing Ronni some blue polish, "true blue for you." The other girls tried to stifle their laughter but couldn't. When Ronni looked at them, confused, Aliya said, "It's nothing, Ronni, just an inside joke we have. Choose whatever color you want."

When it was time to set up sleeping bags, Aliya's mom watched as Aliya put hers in the middle. "Jessica, you be here, Sarah, you be on the other side of me, and Amanda, you be up here by my head." Aliya directed. "Where should I go?" Ronni asked. "Oh. Hmmmm. You can go by my feet." The girls laid out their bags and then walked toward the couch to start watching movies. When Ronni came over, Aliya turned to her. "Ronni, can you go straighten the sleeping bags for a minute? I need to talk to these guys, and it's private. You understand, don't you?" The other girls leaned in around Aliya as Ronni walked over to the sleeping bags, shoulders slumped.

What happened and why?

Nothing feels quite so good as knowing you are "in." And nothing feels quite so bad as knowing you are "out." Because Aliya had felt the latter for so long, she was basking in the joy of finally feeling the former. Previously, her singing had left her on the outside of the social scene, and suddenly it had thrust her into the center! Who wouldn't want that feeling to go on forever? Aliya was in a powerful social position and, like most girls in a similar position, she couldn't help but feed off that power. It was not that Aliya was looking to be mean to Ronni or to actively exclude her. Rather, she was trying to solidify her friendship with the other girls, and Ronni was somewhat of a liability in doing that. Thus, Aliya's actions and comments were not about Ronni, they were about her and her immense desire to fit in, feel powerful, and connect with this new group of friends. Unfortunately for Ronni, one of the most effective ways to fortify a group is to band together against an outsider. And at that moment, at that party, Ronni was that outsider.

What Aliya did well

She pursued her passion: Aliya loved singing and she pursued her passion, even when it got her negative social attention. Knowing this, we can see Aliya's strong inner core and her sense of commitment to something she loves. These are strong character traits that her mother can draw on in this complicated but common social situation.

She stuck with her friendship with Ronni: The truth is, once Aliya was thrust into popularity, it would have been easy for her to blow off Ronni and not invite her in to the recess games. Her allegiance to Ronni up until the slumber party shows that she is a devoted friend who has somehow gotten lost along the way. Again, when parents are able to see the strengths individual girls bring to even frustrating situations like this one, they are in a better position to support their daughters to use these core strengths to feel their power without also hurting others.

Applying the Four Steps: Strategies to use with your own daughter

Staying calm and on your daughter's side is really hard when you see her being mean. The feelings it raises are often multifold: You are worried about, embarrassed by, and, worst of all, distanced from your daughter. When you see your child being victimized, you want to rally around her. When you see her being mean, you want to intervene. Or demand that she change. Or justify the behavior. Or deny it is true. But none of these reactions, as natural as they are, will help your daughter. So what can you do? Take advantage of the Four-Step process!

STEP 1: OBSERVE

Changes, changes, everywhere: We want you to notice and celebrate your child's success and areas of growth, as Aliya's mom did. However, as is true for all girls, along with Aliya's new friends and new attitude came new attention, privileges, and power. Unfortunately, while Mom noticed that Aliya was finally getting the attention and recognition she deserved for her talent and hard work, she did not realize that these types of drastic changes in children's lives—no matter how positive—can also be a red flag. When things change suddenly or dramatically for your child, plug into the Four-Step process to help your daughter develop the skills and maturity to better deal with new circumstances. Because, the reality is, new opportunities also mean new situations that require new skills, and many girls struggle to integrate such immense and sudden changes.

Be a fly on the wall: Anyone who has ever attended girl slumber parties growing up knows, as wonderful as these parties can be, they are also breeding grounds for social cruelty and Mean Girl behavior. Blame it on exhaustion or mob mentality, but parents of young girls should be forewarned that every group sleepover will benefit from parental observation, guidance, structure (!!), and (when necessary) intervention. Here, Mom was given the heads-up before the party that Aliya was not sure how Ronni's presence would mesh with the newly formed clique of the

other girls. Knowing this in advance, she might have pre-
dicted (and helped to prevent) the events that transpired. That
notwithstanding, once the situation unfolded, there were two
ways Mom's observations were needed:

- ❖ In watching the girls set up the sleeping bags, the situation became clear: Instead of one unified group of girls
at a party, there was actually a very split group—
Ronni . . . and the rest of the girls. While it was possible
for Aliya to be the glue to hold things together, at that
moment, there was a sharp division between the girls.
If Mom had noticed this, she would have been ready to
make her next set of decisions.
- ❖ While Mom had been right to want Aliya to include her
loyal friend in the birthday celebration, Aliya was
equally right in saying this party would not be the right
place for Ronni. Hindsight is often 20/20, and given
that Ronni was being targeted and was suffering at the
party, the dynamic as it was playing itself out needed to
change, and fast. The girls obviously needed Mom's
help to do that (see "Support to Act," below, for immediate actions Mom could have taken).

STEP 2: CONNECT

Help her feel great about her recognition: When Aliya began coming
home excited and exuberant about school, new friends, and her
part in the play, Mom could (and should!) have celebrated her
daughter's happiness. It had been a long time coming, and Mom

had undoubtedly seen her daughter's talent forever. Finally it was being valued and appreciated. Allowing your daughter the space to be over the moon about newly won, completely deserved attention will lay the groundwork for any future redirecting that may need to happen, because your child will know you are firmly in her corner, and are as excited about her success as she is.

Honor her frustrations: It is as important to honor frustrations as it is to celebrate successes. Connect (through Active Listening) over the things that drive her crazy or make her furious. Giving her the freedom to vent to you without her feeling like you are getting "preachy" back will have the additional benefit of helping prevent her from wanting or needing to vent with friends (who may use this information against her).

Here, this would have ideally happened *before* the slumber party, which likely would have put Mom on red alert to rethink how she planned the event. However, even after the party, Mom and Aliya could connect about what Aliya had consciously or unconsciously been feeling for a while—that Ronni was being a tagalong with Aliya's new friends.

Parents' first reaction when they see their child act meanly is often to try to swoop in and "fix it," and in certain situations (like this one), intervention may indeed be necessary. However, once any emergency has passed, empathizing with your daughter and showing you understand her perspective, *even if she's being mean,* will more quickly help her find her way back to her core values.

STEP 3: GUIDE

At the slumber party, Aliya's mom witnessed Ronni getting mistreated before her very eyes. Thus, she needed to protect Ronni from further cruelty. To do this, Mom had to support her daughter to act immediately (see Step 4 for how she could do this). After she had put out the fire (and the slumber party had passed), there are a number of ways to guide Aliya:

Feeling it in her core: Mom is in a tricky spot here in trying to guide (and not direct) Aliya. The social interactions young girls are trying to balance are delicate, and unless they themselves feel committed to doing things differently, parental direction will only go so far. That is, while your daughter may do this or that in a particular situation, if she is resistant or defiant to the overall need to interact differently, the effects of any changes will be short-lived and very limited in their scope. Because she will not have learned new skills or new ways to think about and approach these challenging situations, she will not have the internal motivation to make different choices into the future.

So how do you get your child to *realize* she is acting like a Mean Girl? And how do you get her to *want to* change?

- ✿ *Take advantage of the Four Steps*: Let your daughter work through the activities in the Tips for Girls boxes. The exploration and discovery these afford will help her get to know herself better, and will help her make better choices moving forward.

✧ *Work on gaining perspective*: The more ways you can help your daughter put herself in the shoes of a less fortunate individual, and the more you can talk about how she thinks and feels about it, the better. Try following applicable activities:

- Go to an animal shelter or read about the future of a species of endangered animals such as polar bears or sharks.
- Read a book together that explores the topic of mistreatment or injustice. It can be historical (the plight of the Jewish people in Germany, or of Native Americans or African Americans in the United States), or whimsical (the plight of the Truffula Trees in *The Lorax*, by Dr. Seuss, or the troubles faced by the Wumps in Bill Peet's *The Wump World*).
- Watch a movie about a character in a bad situation and talk with your child along the way about identifying with the underdog. For example, watch *Charlotte's Web* and identify with Wilbur. Think also about a story of loyalty and devotion in hard times, such as *The Incredible Journey*, by Sheila Burnford.
- Tell her a story as you snuggle up together. It can be an actual story or one you make up to match the situation she is facing, only with animal characters as opposed to people, to provide a little distance.

✧ *Make it personal*: Help your child be more aware when *she* feels excluded, left out, or abandoned. If your daughter has an older sibling, there are many situations that are ripe for the picking along these lines. Even if your daughter is the oldest or an only child, think about family reunions, holiday get-togethers, or work parties. When your child is in a situation where she is left out, help her pay attention to how she feels, *and then help her connect this feeling to the friend she was cruel to* (for example, ask her, "What do you think Ronni was feeling when you excluded *her* at your party?").

Give her the power: Help your child realize that everyone has been in these situations before, and that she will likely be in them again, many times. However, *each time*, she has the power to be inclusive or exclusive. Emphasize how being inclusive of others makes her powerful. In this way, you can honor the desire for that feeling of power, while at the same time channeling it in a more positive direction.

STEP 4: SUPPORT TO ACT

Break the Mean Girl cycle: The situation at the sleepover required immediate action. Mom needed to step in and help Aliya realize that whatever she was feeling about having Ronni at the party needed to be put aside for the moment. Mom could have said to Aliya that she needed her help in the kitchen and then told her, "I know you are excited to be sharing your birthday with your new group of friends. Ronni is here too. You need to show her some respect. I will help you, but you need to find a way to include—and I mean really include—Ronni." In this way, there would have been no surprises when Mom stepped in with some new activities, and Aliya would have understood in no uncertain terms that she needed to turn things around, quickly, even if she participated somewhat begrudgingly. What activity Mom chose wouldn't have mattered. She was only looking to intervene in the exclusionary chitchatting and then turn the conversation into something more unifying and productive. Some ideas:

❀ *Initiate an individual activity*: If the group is not gelling as a unit, break it apart into individuals as opposed to collections of kids. For instance, you might have the girls make English Muffin pizzas (where each child puts together her own), or set up a sundae bar (where each girl makes her own creation), or get out an art activity (where each girl makes her own sun catcher).

❀ *Initiate a group game*: Unifying the group as a cohesive team is most easily accomplished if the girls have a new common enemy—in this case, someone other than Ronni. So enlist a helpful older sibling, or make it a "kids against parents" activity, or even turn it into a "race against the clock." For instance, how many popcorn pieces can the girls toss into a bowl in sixty seconds?

❀ *Make your presence felt*: Girls are more mindful of their behavior when watchful adults are around. Mill about the living room; notice how girls are seating themselves, to be sure everyone is part of the mix; and help direct the discussion where necessary. Ask the girls questions, talk about interests they share, or get them talking about their favorite TV shows.

> **TEACHER'S Tip:** Individuals Together—Making Pudding
>
> If you notice active and unkind exclusion occurring in your class-room, in addition to addressing the issue with the children involved directly, involve the entire class in an activity that helps students see the importance of individuals in relation to the larger group. One fun way to do this is to make pudding. As you cook, talk about how you need just the right combination of pudding mix and milk to make the mixture hold together smoothly and nicely. Point out how this is simi-lar to how you need the right mix of behaviors to have a class or friendship group work together smoothly. Appreciating every person as an individual who has something to contribute to a group or class allows the school environment to be a positive one.

Three Rs: Once the party was over and things calmed down again, Aliya needed to think about the three Rs (see page 207 for more on the three Rs). And while there were any number of ways to try to rectify this situation, one focus would be on how Aliya planned to do things differently moving forward. She may have chosen to talk to Ronni in person, or initiate the discussion through a letter (that her mom would help her write/edit, to be sure it was appropriate). She might also try to see if the two girls wanted to meet up, with parents along, at a neutral location to try to work things out.

If she is able, it would be nice for Aliya to explain to Ronni how the situation at her party happened: that Aliya was trying to "force" the two sides of herself together, but that she realized that this may not have been the best idea. That she really likes Ronni and values her friendship immensely and does not want

Tips for Girls: If You Think You've Behaved Like
a Mean Girl—Remember the Three Rs

Mistakes happen, and even the nicest person is not nice all the time. Especially if you are often more passive in your interactions (too much of a nice girl), you may find it's really hard to reach that desired "middle ground" of being assertive but not aggressive. So if you find that you have gone too far the other way and are acting like sort of a Mean Girl, forgive yourself:

1. *Recognize* the mistake: Identify the mistake you made, or that you hurt someone.
2. Be *Responsible*: Don't deny it, make an excuse for it, or blame another person (even if you felt pressured by someone else to act in a mean way). Part of making amends is owning your part of what happened, even if others have yet to own theirs. You have the power to stop the cycle. Get help if you need it.
3. *Rectify* what you can: Say you are sorry, listen to your friend's feelings, make an extra effort to show how you have changed or are doing things differently. Tell her what you will do next time, and then check in again to see how she feels now.

"I'm sorry about ___. I think I acted that way because _____. Next time I will___. How are you feeling now?"

Other statements that help resolve conflicts
    Remember: It's as much *how* you say it as *what* you say!

• "I am hoping we can talk about this."
• "Our friendship means a lot to me and I really want to work this out."

- "Tell me more about how you feel."
- "You seem ___. Is there something we can talk about to help things feel better?"
- "I think what I hear you saying is that you don't like it when I do that."
- "I'm not sure I understand what's bothering you. Can you help me understand?"
- "Now I need you to listen to me, please."
- "Help me understand what is making you upset."
- "How can we solve this without calling each other names/ shouting at each other/blaming each other?"

to betray that or lose that, and she knows she did wrong by Ronni at her party. From there she can ask Ronni what *she* thinks they can do to improve the friendship and make it work, thereby showing her willingness to accept responsibility and share the power in the friendship with her friend. Making future plans around an interest of Ronni's might also be a good place to start.

When she's right, she's right: While it seemed very mean for Aliya to say she didn't want to invite Ronni to her sleepover, she actually was right in realizing that this group of friends would not mix well. With Mom's new observations of what was going on for Aliya, and their connections over Aliya's frustrations with Ronni tagging along, Mom could have guided her daughter to think about celebrating her party in ways that would have honored her friendship in different ways. Some ideas:

❖ Increase the group size so that it wasn't one clique of girls plus Ronni, the outsider.

❖ Have two separate parties: one with the clique and then a separate one with Ronni. This additional party does not have to be a big deal—it could be a simple sleepover with Ronni with ice cream sundaes, or even just taking Ronni out to dinner with their family to celebrate Aliya's birthday. So that Ronni would not feel excluded, Aliya could have preemptively told her how excited she was to get to have a private celebration with Ronni alone, as two good friends.

Believe in her: Once you have gone through the Four-Step process, treat your child as if she is already on the path to being able to be kind and make tough social choices. When your child acts meanly, you will likely worry whether your daughter is on a slippery slope to becoming a Mean Girl or a through-and-through bully. Remember, *all* girls can (and will!) act meanly, but that is not to say that your daughter is destined to become a Mean Girl. Therefore, instead of second-guessing if your daughter can or will do a good job being kind, show her you fully believe in her. Doing so will encourage her to be more active and take more appropriate social risks, because instead of seeing a worried, doubting Mom, she can see her biggest supporter cheering her on and knowing she can do it.

TEACHER'S Tip: One for All and All for One

Mobilize your Caring Community to exert positive peer pressure by emphasizing a "one for all, all for one" mantra in your class. Explain to your students that they are all members of this group known as your class, and how each member of the group will get to earn the same positive reward when they work together toward a positive goal. This can be actualized by having them work toward a class pizza party, extra recess time, or the ability to earn a "skip-it" privilege on a test (where each child can choose a problem on the test to have not count toward his/her grade). Talk about how even though not every member of the group might play the same role, or contribute as actively, the band of individuals together working positively makes the group better, and thus each member will earn the same reward. Decide together on behaviors that will earn them the desired "prize," and encourage them to support each other in positive ways to make the goal (for example, having students say to each other, "Come on, let's all sit down quickly, we only have three more stars to earn before our class pizza party!").

You can also use this same framework to emphasize what happens if mob mentality takes over among a faction of students. That is, if some children band together to oust a friend or exclude a classmate, explain that those individuals form a group working toward a negative goal, with each participant suffering the same consequences, regardless of the specific role any individual had taken (overt bully or more passive bystander). Emphasize that individuals always have a choice to walk away, get help, take a stand for peers, and so on. But once they give up their individuality and join a group, they become part of the group decision making, and part of the group outcome—be that positive or negative.

When Girls Struggle with Following the Group

This story highlights the struggles children go through when going along with the group means going against what is comfortable for them. It deals with the times that children ineffectively try and find their place with their group of friends. The story also addresses issues of group ousting, and when girls become Mean Girls in order to fit in. The suggestions apply to scenarios where children are panicked about needing to be different than they are and to follow along with group exclusions in order to stay a member of their group.

Cheerleading performance

Raiden is an athletic sixth grader in Oakland, California. Her school exemplifies the diversity present at many urban schools, and its bully-proofing program is highlighted on its Web page and throughout its curriculum. Raiden's mom had been somewhat surprised at her daughter's new group of friends this school year, because Raiden is a self-identified tomboy, and Tamika, Shannon, Lauren, and Rylee are all "fashion girls" (as Raiden called them). But somehow it all came together and Raiden had never been happier. Until recently.

For weeks, Raiden and her group had been putting together a cheerleading routine at recess. Raiden was excited because her athletic skills made her a leader among her friends. Every day she came home happy and excited, telling her mom stories about the latest moves she developed for the routine, and how they were going to rent the gym to perform for the whole school one evening. They were even going to have their parents buy them matching uniforms.

But recently Mom had noticed a change in Raiden. She had become self-conscious about what she wore to school. She began borrowing items from her older brother, calling even her tomboy clothes "too girly," and so on. One morning, when Raiden was changing her outfit yet again, Mom asked her about it. Raiden brushed her off and headed to school without a smile.

What happened and why?

At this point, Mom was not exactly sure what had happened, but it was clear that something was amiss. By sixth grade, many girls are less open with their parents, especially when the groundwork has yet to be laid with the Four Steps. However, don't mistake this brush-off as Raiden not *wanting* or not *needing* support. Social relationships get more complicated as children mature, and so do their problems. Increasing independence in other areas often leaves eight- to twelve-year-olds feeling they need to better manage their own social lives as well. And while this is desirable, there are many social situations girls can't and shouldn't handle alone. Raiden was in one such situation.

What Raiden did well

She reached out to a new set of friends: While many eight- to twelve-year-olds have a single best friend, these friendships frequently occur within groups. Each new school year often brings a new set of friends to the forefront. While the strongest friendships are usually between girls in the same class, beginning in third grade, some friendships sustain themselves as girls go through the grades, some even as they transition to middle school. This year, Raiden surrounded herself with a new group of very different friends, but found an activity within the group that she enjoyed.

She used a skill to become a group leader: Raiden is very athletic, and among her new peer set this helped her to lead the cheerleading squad. Girls at this age often form friendships based on shared interests and abilities. Raiden's superior skills gave her a leadership role among her group that fed her sense of accomplishment and pride, and solidified her friendship with the girls in her group, despite her being very different from them in other realms.

Applying the Four Steps: Strategies to use with your own daughter

Raiden's mom felt dismissed by Raiden and was unsure how to proceed. While she did ultimately discover the complicated situation Raiden was in (as you will learn below), it took weeks for her to understand what was going on. Forming a plan of action that Raiden could accept also took weeks, as Mom's concern led her to try to take over and fix things. Let's walk through the Four Steps and see how this framework would help you to better support your daughter in these types of difficult situations.

STEPS 1 & 2: OBSERVE AND CONNECT

Mom saw a noticeable change in Raiden's behaviors, a desire for her mother to be less involved in her life, and a change in her mood and affect. As you know by now, these changes are a red flag that something is afoot and a connection is warranted.

Reflect on the information you have: Here, Mom had no idea what happened, but she knew what she had observed. Thus, she could have approached Raiden in a calm, soothing way, to invite her to open up: "Raiden, I have seen a change in you recently. I'm worried about you. Suddenly you don't want to talk about cheerleading or your friends. You seem really stressed about what you wear—I have never seen you need to change outfits five times before you leave for school. I know something is going on and I want us to be able to work as a team to problem solve together. I know you are hesitant to tell me about it, but girls should not have to handle problems by themselves. Let me help you."

Work with what you get: Many times, your first attempt to connect will be brushed off, as your daughter's defenses kick in. Don't be surprised if you hear an attempted distraction coming back at you: "Mom, you always say I should spend more time on my clothes; now I'm doing it! I think you should get off my case." *These moments are when you need to draw on the observations you made during stress-free times*: If your daughter tends to try and push you away when something is bothering her, you know her actions are your signal to try again.

You might be amazed at how effective a gentle response can

be. Think about hugging your child, sitting her on your lap, or rubbing her back. Even sixth graders are comforted by physical proximity. Then add in something like, "I think you're trying to tell me something is going on. I'm here to listen."

Draw on Active Listening, including empathy, regardless of your emotional response: As you saw with Carley, on page 138, some of what your child tells you is happening can be very hard to hear. Your heart may start to race and your blood may boil. But unless your daughter is involved in a perilous situation, or one that requires immediate action, we encourage you to continue to stay calm. Hold yourself back from passing judgment or wanting to take over: Draw on Active Listening and ask questions to fill in the gaps.

In Raiden's case, the group had turned on Shannon, one of the group members, a few weeks earlier. Lauren, the group leader, and Shannon had been best friends, but they had a falling-out, and Lauren had "ousted" her from the group, saying Shannon refused to practice hard enough. Lauren made it clear to the others that when Shannon came over, they were to pretend they were busy talking among themselves, or to walk away. They refused to let her sit next to them at lunch—by either saying the seats were saved or getting up as a group and moving tables. Lauren began telling stories about Shannon, like how messy her house was and how the carpet in her bedroom smelled like dog pee. Raiden had gone along with the teasing and ignoring. She had participated in the gossiping and excluding. She hadn't thought much about it, because she didn't want to lose her group of friends, and she didn't want this "girly social stuff" to mess up the cheerleading performance they had planned. In fact, she secretly noticed that since ganging up on Shannon, the group (minus Shannon) was more united than ever, and that felt good.

Recently, however, Lauren showed them the outfit she had chosen for the performance: a pink, sparkly midriff top with a really short cheerleading skirt—something Raiden wouldn't be caught dead in. The other girls had been excited by the outfit, and so Raiden had feigned liking it as well. Raiden had begun sending nonverbal clues that she was uncomfortable with the outfit, by dressing even more tomboyishly in hopes the girls would see her as athletic. Rather than choosing a new outfit, they just thought she was acting weird. Raiden thought she had seen the others talking about her behind her back. She was getting panicked: "What if they oust me too?" she worried. "What if I have to wear that terrible outfit, just to stay in the group?" Raiden was miserable.

STEP 3: GUIDE

Identify all the issues: A girl will often find herself in complicated situations that only get more complicated when she doesn't reach out for your support and guidance early on. Thus, as we have mentioned, you will benefit from employing the Four Steps *outside* the realm of friendship struggles. You will also want to use them when facing "simple" issues. Doing so will build the framework of support to encourage your daughter to come to you more easily, and to help you better realize, sooner, when things are amiss.

In this situation, Raiden faced several issues: the bullying that was going on between the group and Shannon, the fears Raiden had about being ousted, and her concerns about doing something that made her uncomfortable just to go along with the group.

Scale the worry down to size: As we mentioned previously, children will sometimes make small fears seem very big. Raiden's worry about needing to wear a skimpy cheerleading outfit at some performance the girls were somehow going to set up outside of school was somewhat unrealistic. The reality of the situation was that the performance was probably never going to happen. While Raiden's mom shouldn't belittle the fear Raiden was feeling, she should help Raiden scale this particular worry down to size.

Scale the worry up to size: Raiden's friendship struggles were highly distressing. While she mentioned the relational aggression, social cruelty, and girl bullying somewhat casually, a parent would have likely felt shocked and outraged to hear about the ousting of Shannon, particularly their own daughter's part in it. This meanness is serious business, and you would want your daughter to realize this. However, how you approach this issue makes all the difference.

Rather than lecturing Raiden on what it means to be a friend, her mom would benefit from using Active Listening skills: "How does it make you feel when Shannon comes over and you have to turn away?" "Sometimes laughing together about someone feels like a fun way to connect with friends. Does it feel that way to laugh about Shannon?" "What kinds of things are you thinking when Lauren tells you how you have to act toward a friend?" "Sounds like you think the way the group treats Shannon is pretty terrible, and you are worried they will treat you the same way if you don't wear the outfit," and so on.

Part of scaling this particular worry *up* to size requires helping Raiden think about her fears of being ousted, and allowing that to help her realize what Shannon must have been feeling at the time. She must understand in no uncertain terms that relational aggression, social cruelty, and bullying are never okay, even if she was participating out of self-preservation. However, in order to most effectively help Raiden understand this, her needs and worries—and thus her motivations—cannot be discounted.

TEACHER'S Tip: Supporting "Underlings" in Cliques

When you see the damage a clique can do, it can be hard to know the best way to support the "underlings" in the group. Often they continue to try to be friends with girls who treat them badly. You can say to them, "Based on what I have seen, it seems you are having a hard time with how this group is treating you. Why do you continue to be friends with them?" Once you get past the "they are popular, they are my friends" type of responses, girls will likely talk about the qualities they are looking for in friends. Support them to realize that their group may not be meeting those desires, and ask them how they want to go about addressing that reality.

Present alternative viewpoints:

✣ *The skimpy outfit*: It is hard for young girls not to get distracted by the item at hand (for example, Amelia's crazy socks from page 126). They can miss the bigger picture, whether they are five or twelve. This is why parental guidance is so important. The real issue here was not the outfit but what it was meant to symbolize—that the girls are a team. If Raiden could have helped her teammates feel unified *in a different outfit*, she may have been able to keep her friendship circle and divert the skimpy outfit issue (see "Skimpy Outfit," on page 222, for some ideas on how to do this).

✿ *The cheerleading performance:* The outfit was meant to service the performance, and it seemed likely—given the personality differences—that Raiden and her friends saw the performance as offering them each something different. For Raiden it was about having a forum to showcase her skills—to impress people with her athletic ability. For her "fashion girl" friends, it was likely more about putting on a show with costumes, staging, and attention from an audience. If Raiden could have understood and appreciated how she and her friends were trying to get something different but equally meaningful out of the performance, she could have depersonalized the situation, and possibly could have come up with different ways to meet the same needs (see "Support to Act" for more).

Evaluate the group's actions and her place within it: Part of the struggle for young girls is that their need to belong is so immense, they will often go against themselves or hurt others in order to continue to fit in. Thus, when you guide your child, you need to help her understand the part she plays in the social dynamics, even if she is neither the leader nor the initiator.

With your child, you will want to understand the group and its dynamics. Is this an isolated problem for an otherwise great group of girls? How is conflict handled in the group in general? What are the pairings, and who has excessive power? How are decisions made, and what role does your child tend to have, overall? In this specific incident? In order to help her move forward, make good choices, and make amends, you will need to have a much better sense of the context and dynamics that surround this incident.

Examine the larger context: A bully situation like this requires direct attention. However, unlike what was happening at Aliya's party, Raiden was not involved in a bullying situation that needed an emergency response. Unless urgent action is necessary or your child is in a dangerous or precarious situation, you do not want to take control (and power) away from your daughter by taking over unnecessarily. Not only might this undermine your relationship, but having a parent swoop in and "take over" might make her more vulnerable within her peer group. So, find out as much as you can about the school and its bully-proofing programs, about the social context in the class or the grade, and about the teacher's attitudes toward social issues and those of the other parents involved (see "Talk to the school," on page 225, for more).

The three Rs: Raiden has some reflecting to do. Mom could take advantage of the three Rs and help Raiden realize the ways her going along with the gang has led her to act like a Mean Girl.

Build her self-worth: Girls need to hear over and over, in a hundred different ways, that who they are right now is who they are meant to be. Even if her friends don't understand her, or are jealous of her, your daughter needs to feel that her specialness is not a liability but a strength. She also needs to know that this happens to girls all the time: Friends who might mean well are trying to make everyone exactly alike. And while doing so does not make them bad friends, it does mean that your daughter needs to develop something of a backbone to continue to believe in her own worth, even if she is different from her friends. Or she needs to find the courage to separate herself from her group to find friends who can accept her as she is (see Natasha's story, on page 162).

TEACHER'S Tip: Say It, Mean It

Have Caring Community standards that, when broken, result in consequences. The goal of the consequences is not to stop the cliques or to change a particular child, even if she is a Mean Girl. Rather, following through on expectations will demonstrate to *everyone else* that you mean what you say about not tolerating behaviors that go against your Caring Community. Consequences will empower the bystanders—the silent majority—to know that they can adhere to the standards you espouse because you will as well. What a powerful message to send, even if the bully chooses not to stop!

STEP 4: SUPPORT TO ACT

Become a team: When your daughter is dealing with pervasive bullying issues, it is really important that she feel the two of you are a team facing these conflicts together. Not only will this communicate the seriousness of the situation to her, but it also will help her to know that, whatever happens with her friends, she is not alone.

Find a solution she can live with and feel comfortable about: Finding solutions involves acknowledging that her choices may not be perfect and that she may not be 100 percent happy initially. Getting herself out of a really bad situation sometimes takes time, loss, and struggle, but she will be better off in the long run. This is again where being a team is vitally important.

✿ *Skimpy outfit*: Even though the likelihood of wearing this outfit was small, Raiden still needed to feel proactive about protecting herself:

- Raiden could have suggested a less skimpy outfit that would still have allowed the girls to "dress up" to perform and unify the girls as a troupe. Or she could have suggested they all wear matching comfortable clothes but add pizzazz by getting sparkly batons or flags, or by adding in pom-poms or other fun elements that Raiden would develop into the routine.
- Raiden could have played the "I love the outfits, but my mother won't let me wear such a skimpy skirt" card, with her mom's support.

- She could have tried to change the routine to be very unaccommodating to skimpy outfits and then simply pointed out, "It's just too hard to do the show in these outfits. I think we're going to need to choose something different."

✿ *Fear of being ousted*: Raiden found herself in a very uncomfortable situation with her friends. While it was unlikely that she would decide to walk away from the group immediately, it would have been worth having Raiden (re)discover what true friends are and are not. Unless things with this group turned around, it may have been in Raiden's best interests to ultimately find other friends. Since a girl often feels she cannot walk away from a group of friends however poorly they are treating her, for fear of having no friends, Raiden would likely have needed help to build additional supports while remaining (for a time) a member of her current group:

- *Survey the group*: Is there another friend within the group your daughter could have as an ally? One girl in particular who may have felt similarly, who might have either backed her ideas or "broken away" with her?
- *Look outside the group*: Is there another friend in your daughter's class she can connect with outside of school? In this case, if Raiden could have begun to slowly move away from the intensity of her group, the dynamic might have shifted on its own,

the group may have chosen to more or less drop her without her feeling "rejected," or Raiden may have built up the confidence to make different choices because she was no longer so enmeshed. (For more on how to successfully help your daughter change friendship groups, see Natasha's story, on page 162.)

- *Celebrate differences*: This is a theme you have heard several times. In order for your child to withstand some of the situations she will face in her future, she needs to develop a sense of value in celebrating differences. These differences can be obvious (such as Carley, from page 138, being Japanese American) or they can be hidden. Either way, reading books, telling stories, and setting up experiences to help your child understand and value differences will help her develop self-confidence.

TEACHER'S Tip: Curricular Support for Differences

Don't forget the power of the school in supporting differences, through bully-proofing programs or multicultural curricula that celebrate diversity. You might consider:

- Inviting the school counselor to do an emergency bully-proofing session with your class
- Organizing a class (or even grade-wide) project to highlight the importance of kindness and togetherness

Some possibilities include:

- A unit of study on an endangered species such as sharks. Take a look at savingsharks.com for student and teacher resources, including study guides and volunteer opportunities. When your students band together for a common cause, you engender unity, teamwork, and kindness!
- A project to donate needed items to charity. It can be local or global, such as organizing a shoe collection drive for soles4souls.org, or a similar organization.
- A school mural showing the school's anti-bullying philosophy to be completed in time for "unveiling" at the sixth-grade music program
- A "personal history" journal project where each child interviews a parent about social cruelty s/he experienced as a child. "Publish" it as a class, and have the group present it to the rest of the grade or school at an "understanding bullying" assembly.

Talk to the school: Situations like this are often too big to try to solve at home or with your child alone. Here is a perfect time to show your daughter the difference between telling and tattling. Raiden's school had professed a strong bully-proofing program, and there was a girl in Raiden's group who was hurting others. The teachers needed to be informed, and the school needed to be given the opportunity to work on class dynamics on their end. While you want to be careful that your daughter is not identified/singled out (so she can avoid the social backlash that might cause), you do want to work with the school in forming an alliance against bullying.

TEACHER'S Tip: Approaching Bully Situations—
A Three-Tiered Approach

When you see social cruelty, relational aggression, or bullying going on at school, respond with the following trifold approach:

1. *Demonstrate zero tolerance for bullying.* Inform parents and help separate the group. For example, you might keep the ringleader in for recess ("to help with a project" rather than as punishment) while you encourage the rest of the group to find a new activity to engage in.

2. *Empower the victim.* While the involvement of a school counselor can be very helpful, as the classroom teacher, there is a lot you can do to support a victimized student. For example, encourage her to be a detective and find girls who adhere to the Caring Community standards better. Support her as she attempts to reach out to new friends. Think about allowing her to find a new girl to buddy up with at reading time, or to partner with at science.

3. *Encourage the Caring Community to step up.* Say to your students, "We need to mobilize our Caring Community. I hear there's a group making some of our classmates feel bad . . . what's going on?" Invite the children to speak up and speak out. Then put a charge to them: "Caring Community: are you including these isolated friends? Are you reaching out to them? Without you stepping up and doing the things on our list, we can't be a good class or good school."

★ ☆ ★ ☆ ☆ ★
Walnut Hills 4ᵗʰ graders R.I.S.E. up so that teachers can teach and students can learn
☆ ★ ★ ★ ★☆ ★☆

Classroom Expectations

R — Prepared with materials
— Completes assignments
— Listens and Follows directions
ESPECTFUL — On task
— Respectful to teacher and other students

I — Help others
— Be part of the "Caring Community"
NCLUSIVE — Include people in games
— Invite others to play

S — Keep hands and feet to selves
AFE

E
NVIRONMENT

☆★☆★☆★☆★★☆★☆★☆

Mrs. Stevens starts the year by asking her new fourth graders what classroom behaviors will allow teachers to teach and kids to learn. The children themselves identified that to be Inclusive—a school expectation—they needed to be active members of the "Caring Community," to help others, to include peers in games, and to invite others to play.

Every school in the country has bully-proofing on their agenda. While everyday social struggles and power plays are often ignored, extensive bully scenarios—where girls are locked out of social groups, and group members are forced to exclude, make fun of, or ostracize others—should be taken very seriously, and dealt with very quickly, especially if the issue is raised by a concerned parent. In addition, talking to the school opens the door to additional support for your daughter.

Make amends: We advocate following through on the three Rs by making amends (even in small ways) when your child realizes that her actions have hurt her friend. Here Raiden could have made Shannon an apology card or a friendship bracelet (see "Tokens of friendship" box for more). She could have said she was sorry in person at school, or at Shannon's house, if that felt more comfortable. After apologizing, she could have attempted to reconnect (by having a playdate) or could have allowed time to go by to help heal some of the damage that was done.

Tips for Girls: Tokens of Friendship

There are many things you can do at home, to help rectify a situation privately, before you approach a friend to make amends. For example, you can make a card, bracelet, or friendship pin. When you approach your friend, you can say, "I'm sorry about what I did, and next time I'll do X instead," and you can add, "I hope you know how important your friendship is to me. To show you, I made you this card/bracelet/pin."

7

Think, Share, Do...
Activity Bank for Part II

In continuing this journey with your daughter, you want to build on the rapport and the feeling of safety and comfort you have worked to establish together. The suggestions and activities in this section are organized around the Four Steps: Some activities are carried through across various Steps, some focus on only a single Step. You may choose to do the activities in sequential order or to select ones that are relevant to you. Remember as well that each activity can be modified for both older and younger girls, and can be done multiple times as girls mature.

STEP 1: OBSERVE

Passive, aggressive, or assertive?

One skill you have seen us return to again and again is your daughter's ability to be *assertive,* as opposed to *passive* (victimlike) or *aggressive* (bullylike). While all children can (and will) be all of these at various points in time, your daughter has a *typical* way of interacting with friends. It will be greatly beneficial for you to have a sense of how she interacts with peers, what her response is to conflict, who in her group tends to lead the play, and so on. So the next time your child has a playdate over, or the next time you stay after school so your child can play on the playground, take some time to notice how the interactions unfold. Don't intervene (unless necessary), refrain from commenting, and hold back from guiding. Simply observe, and collect data: What is your daughter's tone of voice saying? What about her facial expressions or body language? Does she make eye contact? Does she tend to lead or follow? Will she offer ideas of her own? Cooperate with her friends' ideas? Take notes as you're watching, if you have to, and try to withhold any judgments, but develop a sense of how assertive your daughter is around her friends.

Tips for Girls: Feeling Powerful

Good friends help you feel happy most of the time, because you know you have influence and power in your relationship. Power is important. Having power means that you feel that your friends take your ideas and the things that matter to you seriously. It is a way of linking your needs and desires with another person's, and finding things to do and say that allow each of you to participate equally. Friendships feel good when everyone has similar amounts of power—when each of you control the play some of the time. But sometimes one girl often has more power than others. This can make friendships feel bad, because one girl is more often controlling the situation and the others just have to go along. To hear stories about friendships where the power isn't equal, ask your parents to share Raiden's story, on page 211; Grace's story, on page 105; or Ellie's story, on page 181.

It is easier to feel powerful if you take some time every day to remember good things. Do this activity every evening and see what a difference it makes. Notice how many times today you say something kind to yourself or to another: "That was a really good idea"; "I am really getting better at reading"; "I was nice to save a seat for Mariela today."

- Write in your journal about three good things that happened to you today.
- Remember one kind thing someone said to you or did for you.
- List five things that are going well for you and make you feel powerful.

Be a fly on the wall

As we suggested in "Aliya's ascent," in chapter 6, Mom could have better contained the cruelty at the slumber party had she been a fly on the wall. This is a tool you can use at home any time. The goal is not to interfere with your daughter's playdates or friendship experiences; it is simply to be present enough that you know the kinds of things that go on in the individual or group dynamics. Observing in this way will give you invaluable information about your child, as well as about the children she chooses as friends. This will help you better connect with her, because you know the players and their personalities. It will also give you additional insight into ways to guide and support your child to act!

> **TEACHER'S Tip:** Be a Fly on the Wall
>
> When possible, be a fly on the wall at recess, in the halls during transitions, or during other unstructured times across the school day. You will be amazed at the information you will gather and the opportunities you will have to prevent social cruelty and bullying!

STEP 2: CONNECT

Valuing persistence

Girls can sometimes feel like the world is ending when they suffer a social setback or a friendship failure. They will often make dramatic, global statements: "I'll never have any friends"; "I'll always be an outsider." Telling them they are wrong often makes them dig in their heels and creates a feeling of disconnection. So engage them in a trip down memory lane. Ask your daughter if she remembers how long it took her to learn to ride her bike, or make it across the monkey bars—and back—or swim the length of the pool, or a hundred other things that took her a great deal of time, energy, and practice to master. Empathize with how hard it is to have to face these challenges. Let her know that you know how it feels to struggle in these ways. Tell her that, just as her other problems were resolved, her friendship struggles will be, too.

If this is not your child's first brush with social setbacks (unfortunately, most girls will experience them multiple times), remind her of previous resolutions. When Reyna's daughter, Natasha, was going through her troubles with Maddie (see "Letting go of a friendship circle," on page 162). Reyna asked Natasha to remember what she did in fourth grade, when her struggles with Jaden began. "I started buddying with Leila for class projects. Then Leila started looking for *me* to buddy with and to play with at recess!" Her confidence renewed, Natasha was more ready to pursue her friendship with Stella's group.

TEACHER'S Tip: Be a Safe Haven

Social struggles will affect all the children in your class at one time or another. Why not offer a temporary safe haven and invite students to stay in and "help you in the classroom" at recess? If students know they can escape the social struggles of the playground for a few days, it may give them just the distance they need to gain perspective. It will also allow you to be a fly on the wall and witness social interactions and kid conversations in action. If you observe that certain students never seem to want to be among their peers or connect in social ways, it may be time to apply the Four Steps to see what larger issues may be at play.

Create "me" journals

To encourage your child to share with you more easily, create side-by-side "me" journals. Make the front cover a self-portrait, and surround it with images of the things you like to do—the things people who see you from the outside would notice (you like swimming, photography, and so on). Explain that these journals now show the outside of yourselves—what others see. Comment that the insides are things others will see only if we show them. Have your child paste in images of things about her that are private, special, or known only by a few people. She can write thoughts, feelings, and fears as well. Use the books to talk about yourselves. What is important to you? Why is something a favorite? Remember to use Active Listening as your daughter shares this more personal side of herself. Encourage her to continue working on the inside of her journal. Be sure you follow suit and share some of the things that are special or private about you, including additional entries to model how to use the journal as a place to reflect on experiences or conflicts.

Connecting together

While you learned a great deal about the struggle Raiden had in trying to remain a member of her friendship circle, you learned only a little about her friend Shannon's situation. Shannon, like many girls her age, was not only ousted from her group but repeatedly subjected to acts of social cruelty and bullying. And parents are sometimes the last to learn of their daughter's struggles. The following ideas may help facilitate the dialogue to help your daughter open up more easily, and sooner, if she is in a similar situation:

Enjoy a hobby together: Let your daughter know what a fun and wonderful person she is by carving out some "girls only" time. Let her lead the activity and teach you about something that is important to her, or engage in a shared hobby. If, during the course of your shared activity, the conversation naturally turns to her current friendship worries, that is fine. However, remember that the goal here is first and foremost to connect.

TEACHER'S Tip: Connecting with Students

As a teacher, you can greatly influence a girl's sense of self in many small ways. For example, pull out a book and offer it to her, telling her, "I saw this book and it made me think of you. I know you really like fairies and I thought this would be a great one for us to read together during silent reading time!" You can do this type of connecting with any number of students across the year, so none of the children feel you have favorites.

Be direct: Sometimes, we only ask the tough questions during tough times. Why not set up a time when things are calm to take a leisurely walk with your child? Simply ask her how she feels about her friends these days—whom has she been playing with, what do they do? See what she is feeling good about, and what she wishes were different. Use Active Listening and just follow her lead.

STEP 3: GUIDE

Bravery Book

It is often very hard for girls to know that talking about their social struggles is a brave thing to do. They can feel that they should be able to solve their problems on their own, or that their worries (while feeling overwhelming to them) will seem irrelevant to their parents. Thus, the more you convey how important it is for your child to share her struggles, and how brave it is to try to face them in new ways, the more she will come to you in times of stress or need. Think of Hailey's story, where it took days and finally a confrontation from Mom for Hailey to share her worries over her break with Ellie.

When something like this happens in your own family, take advantage of the opportunity it presents:

- ❖ Write a Bravery Book about the incident, celebrating how much it took for your daughter to confide in you, and how brave she was to reach out to friends in new ways. Type it up on the computer, and leave blank space for your daughter to illustrate it. Staple it in bookbinding format and read it as a family over dinner.
- ❖ Or make a book about *all* the ways your daughter is brave, without focusing on a single incident.
- ❖ You can also print out (or purchase) an award certificate or get a first-place ribbon or medal. Have a small ceremony in which you present the award to your child: "for being brave," "for reaching out," "for making new friends"—or any other related achievement that you want to highlight and celebrate.
- ❖ Think about asking at dinner each night, "What was one brave thing you did today?"

Don't forget to have everyone in the family participate in answering!

By helping your daughter reflect on and feel proud of her brave actions, you are guiding her to notice and appreciate an important aspect of herself. As her sense of bravery becomes more ingrained, she will be better able to feel and act bravely when interacting with her friends.

Proud yet humble

"Retaliatory" behaviors can begin early—think of Rachel in Maya's story, who in kindergarten went on the attack after she felt embarrassed by Maya's comment about her cursive-writing ability. Thus, your daughter will benefit from your guidance to help her interact with friends in ways that don't lock out friendship or cause girls to turn on her out of jealousy or perceived humiliation. Think of your daughter's talents. In Reyna's family, it was Natasha's skill in math; in Michelle's family, it was Kylie's talents in the arts. Then role-play with your child to help her learn how to accept compliments while *also* complimenting back. Even if your child's friends are not jealous of her or acting out against her because of her talent, offering and accepting compliments is a learned skill that will take your daughter far (see "Connect with compliments," below, for more).

For example, when Aliya's friends came up to her after the school play when she was the lead, it took practice to comfortably accept her peers' admiration and then also congratulate them on a job well done by saying something like, "Thanks so much. And thanks also to you! There is no way I could have learned my lines if you hadn't helped me." Or, "Thanks! I loved when you threw the water at Miss Hannigan! That really made the show!" Accepting praise and then commenting on or asking about others' strengths and interests will help your daughter's friendships to grow, and it will help mitigate group conflict and misunderstanding.

TEACHER'S Tip: Learning to be a Leader

Knowing how to be part of the group is vital to making and keeping good friends. Paul Von Essen, the Littleton, Colorado, social worker and national speaker on bully-proofing, helps students learn how to be part of the group beginning in third grade. He teaches them the skills to be productive, contributing members of both social and "academic" groups. As he describes it, "Learning to be in charge and be a good leader comes out of being a good group member, as opposed to the other way around, as many think." So if you hear girls complaining about "bossy" children, take the opportunity to redirect this tendency to be bossy, and teach your class the ways that successful group membership helps develop leadership skills! Another way to support leadership abilities is to run a leadership training program during recess, develop a peer mediation program, provide rotating class leadership opportunities, or assign "middle-of-the-road" girls to be class buddies with girls who are struggling socially.

Talking in generalities

Although gossiping and venting about other girls can be an effective way to connect, it is also more than likely going to get your daughter in trouble in her friendship circle. One way to guide your daughter is to give her additional means that serve the same end, such as discussing the *traits* of a friend in a *general* sense *without* actually talking *about a specific girl*. Help your daughter realize she can still connect with a friend; they can talk about how they both hate bossiness, without having to say they hate how bossy Sally is.

For example, model this by pointing out how annoyed you are when people are late, without mentioning Aunt Clara by name. Or "catch yourself" naming names and correct yourself in an obvious way for her. To take an example from Michelle's home, where her husband, Scott, has a new job a long distance away, Michelle has "caught herself" saying: "Argh! Daddy makes me so mad! I hate it when he says he'll be home for dinner, but then stays late for another meeting! Um. Well. Actually, I feel disappointed when I'm excited to get to see Daddy, and then his work makes me have to wait longer than I want to. It's super-frustrating!" Modeling in this way allows your daughter to see how to identify the actual emotion behind the anger (disappointment or sadness), and puts her in a better position to talk about it openly.

Even young girls are capable of describing complex emotions and reflecting on difficult situations. In this case, six-year-old Maya writes a letter to Michelle describing how she feels after Michelle told Maya she did not believe her version of an incident between Maya and Bryce. It reads, "I thought that you believed everything I say and never said, 'I don't believe you.' We are a family that believes in each other. PS: I'm very sad you said that. I hope you and me can communicate. I hope you can make a choice to believe me. I can't wait to hug again. Sincerely, Maya."

Spend the next week working as a team and write down the things that frustrate your child. Any- and everything! Then go through the list and see what universal characteristics are hidden in the complaints.

Erasing the hurt

Girls often act without realizing the effect their actions or words can have on others. You can make this idea visual and concrete with this simple activity:

⚜ With a dark pencil, have your child write the words "hurt feelings" in large letters on a piece of paper. Point out that when people say mean things to people, it leaves them with hurt feelings.

⚜ Ask her if those words will erase themselves if left there for a long time (no). Ask her, "How can we erase these hurt feelings?" She will likely say, "By using an eraser." You can agree by saying, "Yes, the 'eraser' we can use to help get rid of these hurt feelings is to say we're sorry: 'I'm sorry I hurt your feelings.'"

⚜ Erase the words, noticing together how, even when you tried to erase the hurt feelings, they are still there, even though they look lighter. Explain to her that even when you try to erase mean behavior (by apologizing, for example), some of the other person's hurt feelings still remain.

⚜ You may also choose to write specific emotions, like "sad" or "embarrassed," as opposed to the words "hurt feelings."

> **TEACHER'S Tip:** Erasing the Hurt
>
> The activity above is a great one to do with an entire class—either at the beginning of the school year, when laying down the class rule of "being kind" (so that kids see concretely why that rule is so important), or later in the year, if your class is struggling with treating one another respectfully.

> **Tips for Girls:** Words Leave a Hole
>
> Get a piece of Styrofoam and poke your pencil or a golf tee into it. Even when you take the pencil or golf tee out, there is still a hole. This is the effect that mean words or unkind acts have on others. The words (like the pencil or tee) may be gone, but the hole left in the other person is still there.

STEP 4: SUPPORT TO ACT

Identifying manipulation in yo-yo friendships

As you saw in the situation between Grace and Ashley, one of the challenges in dealing with a yo-yo friendship is that the less powerful girl is often complicit in allowing the relationship to continue. Most girls in this situation have a very difficult time understanding that they are indeed being bullied. To them, bullies are people who set out to hurt others on purpose; a bully is not your best friend who stands up for you, laughs at your jokes, and shares your interests and passions.

Because it is so difficult for the more passive girl to pull herself out of a yo-yo friendship, the first step she must take to protect her own well-being is to recognize her friend's manipulation. Therefore, you are in a position to support your daughter to act by helping her to recognize the behaviors her friend is engaged in, without necessarily labeling them as "bullying." Your daughter will, over time, be in a more powerful place to separate from the destructive relationship.

If she is ready to begin the initial phase of the journey, talk together about the ways people can manipulate others, without forcing them or "bullying" them, but still getting the other person to more or less do what they had wanted all along. Have your daughter make a list: How does your daughter's friend get her to make the choices she does? Does she cry? Make her feel guilty? Threaten to end a playdate? Imply the loss of the friendship? If your daughter can begin to identify the ways in which she is being manipulated, cajoled, or even tricked into feeling okay about choices that actually leave her feeling bad, she has made the first active step to moving in a new direction. This is a way of helping your daughter to ask herself, "How do I have control in my own relationships? How can I 'be somebody' while remaining true to myself?" As she reflects on these questions, she can write down her answers (or have you write them) to come back to at other points in navigating the yo-yo friendship.

She can also list the qualities she would like in a friend or a best friend, along with those she would find in a "no-friend." Which list contains more qualities that apply to her friend? If her yo-yo friend possesses a lot of the good qualities, recognize that, but also help her to tangibly see how many are also on the "no-friend" list. Help your child make a list of her other friends. What makes each person a good friend? Think about and discuss her choices in friends. Now, check yourself: Do you know each of these children? Their parents? Think about the role you can play in supporting your daughter as she branches out in different ways.

Becoming more assertive

Children often feel vulnerable in social interactions with peers and friends. So why not take advantage of alternative venues to develop her assertiveness? Asking for help, participating in a new activity, sharing her ideas, and stating her limits are all assertive acts, so support your child to choose some venues to give it a try. When Kylie was recovering from surgery, she was out of the pool for almost a month. Upon returning to swim team, she was noticeably weaker. However, the new coach did not know why she had been away and insisted that she keep up with the other swimmers. After looking over to Michelle helplessly, she put on her assertive face, threw back her shoulders, and explained to the coach just what she and Michelle had practiced: "I just had surgery. I need to take it slow, so I am going to sit this one out. When I catch my breath, I will be ready to swim again." The coach nodded and started the other swimmers; Kylie joined back in on the next set.

When you support your daughter in developing her assertiveness, think about stacking the deck in her favor. Like Michelle, you can role-play with your daughter so she is confident in what she will say, or you can talk to the important players beforehand. For example, if she is going to assert herself by participating more at school, let the teacher know the additional motive for your daughter's increased hand-raising. This will help you and the teacher to work as a team on your daughter's behalf, and it will better guarantee that your daughter gets called on (and thus sees herself as *successful* at asserting herself).

TEACHER'S Tip: Recognizing Assertiveness

Whenever you see a student step out of her comfort zone or attempt to master a new skill, be sure to give her recognition. Recognize a child's assertive acts at a class meeting. ("I have noticed that Rose is working hard to speak louder in class so we all can hear her. This is an example of what it looks like to "be brave" in class.") This will encourage all the children to stretch themselves beyond their comfort zone.

Plan B

As you saw in both Maya's and Hailey's stories, girls oftentimes feel ostracized and alone as a result of a social issue. Given that these issues arise quickly and mostly without warning, it may be useful for your child to feel like she has ready access to a Plan B, should she feel isolated as a result of some sort of social fallout. To do this, support your child in collecting items to keep in her backpack, to bring out to the playground (if allowed) on a particularly hard or lonely day. This will give your child something in her "back pocket" to play with by herself (a deck of cards, a jump rope), or to use to engage another child. Even if the school has balls or ropes, something brought from home is new and automatically interesting, and it may be just what your child needs to form a new connection, or at least to feel like she is engaged as opposed to alone. Small, portable items you might consider include a Chinese or regular jump rope; jacks; travel dominoes (or other travel games); small notebook (or two) and a pencil or small markers to draw with or to use for tic-tac-toe or hangman; deck of cards; cat's cradle string; and so on.

Even at only five years old, Reyna's daughter Nadia was very adept at creating her own Plan B. For days, the girls had been playing a game that she didn't like. On her own initiative, she brought in a CD for show-and-tell and asked her teacher to play it during free time. Starting the CD was a way to invite the other girls in to a new interaction that Nadia thought was fun too!

We are alike, we are different

No matter what her background, your child will need to deal with diversity as she learns to make and keep friends. One way to broach this topic is to explore how even in her own family, every person is unique. With an inkpad, have each person place a thumbprint in the center of a piece of light-colored paper. Using a magnifying glass, examine how the thumbprints are alike and how they are different. Talk about how even on this very basic level, we are individuals and we express ourselves in our own special ways. Demonstrate this by having each person independently create her own thumbprint animals. Come back together and see what you have each created.

TEACHER'S Tip: Squiggles

Draw an interesting squiggle on a piece of paper. Photocopy one for every class member. Without looking at another's work, have each child turn the squiggle into a design of her own choosing. Share each with the class. How different are they? Are there any similarities across the differences (everyone drew with markers, half the class did animals)? How are any similar ones still different? Extend the activity by having your students bring home a blank page with the same squiggle for their parents, without sharing what they did at school. Have the parents send in their designs and have the class compare these to their child's. How are they alike? How are they different? This might be a fun display for back-to-school night or to introduce the topic of celebrating differences in your class.

Trying new things

Your child will be much more comfortable with accepting diversity among her friends if she knows you are as well. Think about getting a book about a different culture and reading it together. Ann Morris has a lovely photographic series on a number of topics (bread, homes, loving, shoes, hats). The books show each of these items in use in various cultures. Talk about how the items or experiences depicted are the same as and different from your own family's. If you get a book like *Bread, Bread, Bread*, take a family field trip to a bakery and have a conversation about diversity while you all try out some of the different kinds of doughy options, including those from other cultures!

> ### TEACHER'S Tip: Exploring Differences
>
> ||||||||||||||||||||||||||||||||||||||||||||||||||||||||||||||||||||||||||||||||||||||||||||||||||||||||||||||||||||||||||||||||||||||||||||||||||||||||||||
>
> Even if you have a seemingly homogeneous class, explore the diversity that exists. Think family structure, style of living (home, apartment), learning styles, and so on. Get creative in how you have the students explore and discover similarities and differences among the group. When Michelle's daughter Kylie was in first grade, each student made a poster of her cultural heritage and family practices. Up until then, Kylie had felt different because she is vegetarian. But that feeling disappeared when her friends gobbled down the veggie-chicken nuggets she brought in as part of her poster presentation!

Connect with compliments

Everyone needs a means to connect. Unfortunately, most girls tend to connect with other girls by gossiping or talking negatively about outsiders. Doing so solidifies them as a coherent unit: an "us" against a "them." However, it is possible to change this mentally—to *connect through compliments*. The compliments become the glue that solidifies the "us" *without needing to have a "them."* Giving compliments is a skill in and of itself, and it is one you can help your child learn in playful ways!

Michelle's five-year-old daughter Maya struggled with learning to be a good sport (see "Let the Games Begin," page 56). The skill she learned for game playing was also useful in learning how to build connection through noticing another's skill. For example, when Michelle and Maya beat Granny Annie and Kylie in a game of foosball, our natural inclination was to high-five each other and celebrate.

But it was *Maya* who noticed the despairing look on eight-year-old Kylie's face and instead said, "Wow, guys, that was a great game. You really played your hardest and you did a great job. I bet you'll win another time." In an instant, Kylie's disappointed look melted away. She felt part of the "in" group again (the group that tried hard and did well). What a difference it made for the focus to be on the shared experience of the whole group, as opposed to the divisive celebration of the two winners!

You can also build these skills midgame. Encourage your child to compliment her teammate (and opponent!) when she makes a good move or a great save, for example. If you switch the emphasis to positive reinforcement (instead of the "Argh! You let her score a point! Watch the goal!" kinds of interactions), you will find that in no time at all, these ways of working together are natural at home, and with peers. Even two-year-old Bryce can be heard saying happily, "Nice shot!" after one of his sisters *misses* a basket, and we have no doubt you too can *connect with compliments*.

Empowering ostracized girls

Both Raiden and Shannon experienced extreme stress as a result of friendship struggles that left them feeling disconnected from their entire network of love and support. Thus, reconnecting girls to their family and helping them build up other avenues of support is vital, especially for girls like Shannon, who were subjected to group ridicule and humiliation for a significant period of time. If your child is trapped in an ongoing bully situation, be sure to take action and look at the suggestions offered in Natasha's story (page 162), Grace's story (page 105), and Raiden's story (page 211), in addition to the ideas below:

❖ Have your daughter plan a family activity that she looks forward to, or remind her of one that is coming (for example, if you are going to the mountains, let her plan the day at the Alpine Slide). Invite her to help make a list of things to do to get ready. Giving her control over elements of her experience, and building excitement about aspects of her life outside of school, will help balance out the pain she may feel with her friends.

❖ Support your daughter to enact (privately) what she *wishes* she could say to her friends. Allowing her a release for her frustration will give her the means of "confronting" her peers without needing to actually do so. She can do this through role-playing, with puppets or other figures, through a letter she never sends, and so on. Often girls need to release the anger, sadness, or embarrassment before they are able to move on to more outward and appropriate ways of making connections with friends (such as trying to call an old friend on the phone or approach a new friend at school).

Imagine the worst: Sometimes girls are hesitant to act more bravely because they worry about the worst. Rather than try to convince your child otherwise, support her to think through, or act out, the worst-case scenario. When Michelle's daughter Maya wanted to audition for a Missoula Children's Theatre show, she almost didn't go through with it because she was too scared. So Michelle supported Maya to walk through the worst-case scenario:

- ❖ "The worst thing would be if I forgot my lines." What would happen then?
- ❖ "The kids might laugh." What would happen then?
- ❖ "I'd be embarrassed." What would happen then?
- ❖ "If I was embarrassed . . ." Maya couldn't finish the sentence, which brought her worry down to size. She auditioned for the play, got a part, and had the time of her life. Even though her bunny ears fell off in the middle of a dance number, she had realized that her worst-case scenario really wasn't that bad!!

Have a party for no reason at all (or create a reason!): Setting up a playdate can be difficult if your daughter is still reeling from her group ousting. So help her take the pressure off of trying to form new connections and support your daughter to find a reason to celebrate nothing! When Kylie was preparing to change schools before third grade, she invited all the nine-and-under girls on her swim team to an ice cream sundae party at Red Robin's. Doing so made her the center of attention, gave her a forum to meet

---

Tips for Girls: A "Can" Can

Setting goals and achieving them is the result of a lot of hard work! One way to tangibly see your efforts rewarded is to make a "can" can. Get two unbreakable jars, small boxes, or other type of holders. Decorate them both, labeling one with the word "Goals" and the other with the word "Can." Write out a number of your goals on strips of paper, and place them in the "goal" can. They can range from relatively "small" ones (like remembering to take out the garbage or learning to jump rope twenty times) to big ones (like auditioning for a lead in the school play). When you have accomplished your goal, move the strip of paper from the "goal" jar to the "can" can as a concrete way to celebrate your accomplishment!

and connect with new girls, and gave her an unpressured environment in which to befriend new girls.

Accepting responsibility

No one wants to admit she has done something wrong, or to have to apologize for hurting another person. Help your child understand that every time she accepts responsibility for her mistakes, she grows up a little bit on the inside. Tell her the story of George Washington and the cherry tree, being sure to include the details about why he told (according to some stories, because his father was going to punish the slaves for the tree's felling). Having discussions about issues such as this one gives your child an

TEACHER'S Tip: Historical Stories

Obviously, there are many opportunities to use historical stories in an educational setting. The new spin is to open the possibility of a moral discussion, where you welcome various views on a topic. What better way to model an acceptance of differences! Be sure you point out to your students how part of creating a Caring Community involves welcoming a variety of ideas.

opportunity to talk about where she is in her sense of moral duty. Be sure you ask questions, employ Active Listening, and provide your child ample opportunity to lead the conversation rather than simply listen to you preach.

Combating loneliness

Stories are a powerful way to help girls connect to their emotions, talk about tough issues, and realize they are not alone. When girls identify with characters in novels, it provides the perfect framework to talk about issues, without having to take them so personally. For example, read *Island of the Blue Dolphins*, by Scott O'Dell aloud together. See if your daughter can take the lead in discussing what Karana might be feeling, alone on the island for all those years. There are many compelling stories that will help you to approach friendship issues.

TEACHER'S Tip: Asking for Help

If you read books that highlight friendship struggles aloud in class, have students suggest ways to deal with their feelings, including asking for help. When Mrs. Lienemann, Kylie's third-grade teacher, openly discussed children being assertive in seeking help, students responded enthusiastically. While some asked for help with things like decimals, one child asked for help making new friends. When Mrs. Lienemann asked, "Who here is willing to be friends with Sammy?" every single hand in the class went up. For over a week, Sammy bounced in from recess, delighted that if one group of friends didn't open the doors to the play, there were other options to be pursued!

Wrapping up

Using the Four Steps in Your Home, School, or Office

There are so many changes your daughter will go through between the beginning of kindergarten and the end of sixth grade, the age range highlighted in this book. Who your child is and how she confronts and deals with social struggles will undoubtedly change many times. Rather than feel like each social "emergency" is a new, never-been-dealt-with-before issue (some in fact may be), let the Four-Step plan allow you to feel like an expert: a skilled, seasoned *observer*, a compassionate, understanding *teammate*, an experienced, professional *guide*, and a responsive, knowledgeable *supporter*.

Through this process you can move from isolated incidents to an understanding of who your child is in the world and how she approaches conflict and confusion, and you can support her growth and development toward maturity. You can work to *prepare* her rather than trying to (unsuccessfully) *spare* her. In this way, rather than feel as if you and your daughter are drowning in still waters, with the aid of the Four-Step program, you can stand along the shores or wade in up to your ankles and watch (with new eyes) as your daughter enters social waters and learns to swim on her own. And, importantly, you are *not only there, but you are the one she turns to,* to buoy her up and to support her in finding a seaworthy vessel. You are there, *and the one she turns to,* to guide her as she navigates the stormy seas of friendships lost or found, betrayed or renewed.

Of course, the "what" and "how" of this guidance and support will likely change from situation to situation. However, the foundation offered through the Four Steps will stay with you and will work for the myriad situations your daughter encounters as she develops, and with her growing and changing set of skills. She will feel the strength of your connection and the power in her own abilities as she makes choices that are based on a better understanding of herself and her peers. These new skills and ways of relating will benefit you both well into the teen years, so continue to draw on the Four-Step process throughout middle school!

The Difference Between "Younger" and "Older" Girls

Taking advantage of the Four-Step plan will help you to work at your child's developmental level, whatever it may be. According to social worker and national bully-proofing expert Paul Von Essen, most younger girls—those in grades K–2—are just trying to figure out what to do in the school environment (both socially and academically) and how to "be somebody." For most girls this age, actions stem from egocentrism, resulting in decisions made with mainly themselves in mind. This means that there is rarely malicious *intent* to hurt their friends or peers. Of course, hurt feelings often arise—because girls this age are not able to fully consider the other child's point of view and because they cannot fully appreciate the effects of their actions (or preview them well). Therefore, the first few years of school are a time of learning to manage the desire for social power, as opposed to acting with malicious intent.

By third grade (earlier for some girls!), children are more sophisticated, and we begin to see social manipulation and the formation of cliques. It is during this time that a larger number of individual children are looking to "run the show." As a result, children engage in more traditional forms of bullying and social cruelty, and we see a manifestation of the true intent to hurt, harm, embarrass, or exclude. Thus, from third grade onward, children benefit from a better understanding of how to be a productive group member, as opposed to acting on the impulse to try to be the group leader. As we have mentioned, learning to be in charge and be a good leader comes out of being a good group member, as opposed to the reverse.

Not Racing to Grow Up

Each child is on her own path to maturity and may show more sophistication in some areas, and less in others. This "unevenness" in development is both normal and expected. If your daughter seems in a race to grow up (you observe that she wants to wear provocative clothes, begins rolling her eyes at you, and so forth), try not to panic. Most girls are simply trying out social roles that they are eager to grow into. Draw on the Four-Step plan and think of her new ways of interacting as an invitation to begin discussions around important issues. To help her enjoy the wonders of the age she is:

Connect: Draw on Active Listening to find out more about what her friends are wearing/doing. Let her know that *together* you will decide on family expectations about ways of communicating and the clothes and makeup she wears out of the house, now and in the future.

Guide: Help her understand that as girls mature, the responsibilities and the pressures they face multiply. When girls try to look or act older, they often have to face these pressures when they are not ready to handle them, and shouldn't have to. Together, create a list of ways she can appropriately explore these natural desires.

Support her to act:
- ✤ *Support an outlet*: Give her permission to try on different roles within the safety of your home by having makeup, dress-up clothes, and fun hair supplies she can experiment with.
- ✤ *Support an action*: Together notice the positive actions of teenagers, and find age-appropriate ways to encourage her to do the same: make her own lunch, walk home from school with a friend, keep track of her own

belongings. Sometimes girls are in less of a hurry to grow up when they realize the additional demands and responsibilities that come with it!

Facing All Kinds of Issues, Together

Through observing "where she is," or what her struggles and strengths are, you are in the best position to connect with your daughter. By drawing on stategies such as Active Listening and Sharing Stories, you and your child will become a unified team, facing friendship issues together. Through the strength of your alliance, you will be able to guide your child—helping her better understand herself and her peers, appreciate various viewpoints, and open herself up to trying new strategies or reframing problems. She will also be better able to understand and reflect on her place in her social circle and friendship pairs. Through your interactions around these issues, you can help her see "little problems" as *big enough* to seek connection over. On the flip side, in guiding your daughter, you can help her realize that some problems that *feel* big really aren't as overwhelming when faced with a knowledgeable and supportive ally.

Each "new struggle" can be met in a familiar way, and your child can learn how to respond more easily because you and she will consistently reinforce ways of interacting that work to her benefit. You will be able to fine-tune those that do not. In this way, the Four-Step plan will provide a framework where your child knows you are there to celebrate her abilities, understand her worries, and guide her to feel her own power and make her own choices. Drawing on this framework in all kinds of situations, not just social struggles, will encourage your child to come to you with *all* her emotions—happy, proud, sad, worried, confused, and so on—which will then leave you in the best position to guide her and support her to act.

All along the way in the Four-Step program, we help you empower your child. Very often, children experiencing social struggles focus their energy on getting the other child to stop whatever the offensive or destructive behavior is—to somehow get the other child to change. Unfortunately, this expectation leaves your child powerless in that it is not possible to ensure that another individual change, no matter how much your child may wish she would. The emphasis of the Four Steps is on helping you and your child better understand the context of social struggles, your child and the other child's role in that context, and the series of choices *your child has*, regardless of what the *other child* may do.

When Paul Von Essen talks about this topic with the students he works with, he asks them: "What will you do if the bully never stops? What words can you say to yourself, what actions can you take for yourself if the bully never stops?" For some, particularly younger children, there will likely be more adult involvement. As children develop, the answer to these questions needs to come more from an internal set of skills that have been (and continue to be) supported and fostered over time. The Four-Step program is the answer for girls at any and every age, because it gives girls choices that are built on what they themselves are able to enact at any given moment in time, in the myriad situations they are likely to face.

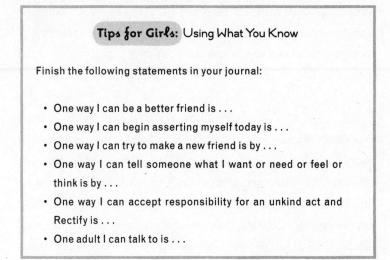

Tips for Girls: Using What You Know

Finish the following statements in your journal:

- One way I can be a better friend is . . .
- One way I can begin asserting myself today is . . .
- One way I can try to make a new friend is by . . .
- One way I can tell someone what I want or need or feel or think is by . . .
- One way I can accept responsibility for an unkind act and Rectify is . . .
- One adult I can talk to is . . .

However, it is important to realize that even if you do everything "right," your daughter will not learn these lessons instantly. Development, by definition, is a process of change over time, and it takes many experiences for girls (and adults!) to integrate new ways of approaching and understanding experiences. Be patient with the process and allow each of you to make mistakes along the way.

As much as you might wish, you cannot make your daughter's friends be kind, include her, tolerate her limits, or like her. You cannot stop the all-too-common pressures, hurt feelings, exclusions, and "dumpings" from happening. And there may in fact be situations so destructive, debilitating, or dangerous that measures beyond which are covered in this book are necessary.* But,

---

*If your daughter or any child you know is in a situation that is beyond her control or one that threatens her or another's safety or well-being, act immediately and involve the proper authorities right away!

most of the time, the Four Steps will allow you and your daughter to better understand, confront, manage, and mitigate friendship struggles, relational aggression, and bullying.

She Is Not Alone

One reason for you to invest in the Four Steps while your child is young is to allow you to be a strong ally in helping her depersonalize friendship issues and social cruelty, thus allowing her to know that she is not alone, and that she has support. So many young girls keep their sadness and worries over these issues as hidden as they can, for as long as they can. When they do talk about them, girls often present their worries in watered-down and glossed-over "she was mean" types of reporting. Not realizing just how important and devastating the happenings actually are for their child, parents often unwittingly brush these scenarios off with "she'll be nicer tomorrow" types of responses. Unfortunately, such situations often distance girls from the adults who care about them, distract girls at school, and over time can cause depressed moods, explosions at home, and/or decreased self-esteem.

Happily, when you apply the Four-Step program and begin these discussions in the early years—while your daughter still looks to you for guidance and welcomes your input in her life— you can more easily help her feel powerful as she acts and responds to social struggles and Mean Girl behaviors well into middle school. In addition, it will help her understand that there is nothing wrong with *her*, and that these are situations every girl must confront.

Whether you are a parent, a counselor, or a teacher—we hope

that *Little Girls Can Be Mean* has given you four simple Steps to use in approaching friendship issues, as well as specific tools and strategies to help the girls you care about learn to deal with situations of social cruelty. Through the use of the Four Steps, you will help bolster and strengthen the girl you love, making her stronger, more resilient, and better able to stand up for herself right now and in the years to come.

Appendix 1

Bully Stories for Home or School

Discuss the following stories and apply the Four Steps or use them as a basis for role-playing at home or in school. Some questions to think about asking: Is this situation an example of bullying? Why or why not? Imagine your child or student came to you and told you about the girl described. Is this a situation in which to apply the Four Steps? Why or why not? What would each Step look like in this situation?

Linda Leader

Linda likes to be in charge. She is always the first one to raise her hand, offer an answer, volunteer to help out, and rush to get on line. She is also the first person to offer to help you if you don't understand something in school, and she always lets you in her games. She might say, "Sure, you can join in. You be the little girl and I'm the mommy, and Caitlin is the teacher. Let's play that I come in for a parent/teacher conference." Is Linda acting like a bully?

Kathy Computer

Kathy is great on the computer. She can type her school reports now and has her own e-mail account. She likes to send you instant messages. You're not that good on IM, but it's fun to chat over the computer. One night, you get an IM from Kathy about a Web posting. "Look what Tally got on her science assignment!" it reads. You go to the posting and see a copy of Tally's science report with red marks from your teacher splashed across it. You know that Kathy and Tally are friends, and that Tally must have shown her report to her. But how and why did Kathy post it on the Web? Is Kathy acting like a bully?

Three's a Crowd

You and Claire have been best friends for months now. In the last few weeks, she has also been wanting Lizzie to play with you guys at recess and sit with you at lunch. You like Lizzie and have been having a great time. Recently, Claire and Lizzie have been going off together at lunch without you. Sometimes you move your stuff to be with them, sometimes you eat with the other kids who happen to sit at your table. For the last few days, when you go over to join them at recess, Claire has said, "I hope you don't mind. I just want to play with Lizzie alone again today." Is Claire acting like a bully?

Stephie's Secrets

You have been best friends with Stephie for almost the whole school year. But after a recent fight, she began spending her time with Allison. They made a "friend notebook" that they bring to recess. They talk about things they've done together without you, and you feel left out. A few days ago, Allison ran out to recess (where you and Stephie were together) and handed Stephie some notes, telling her not to show them to anyone. Then they walked off together. You could tell they didn't want you around. Later, you talked to Stephie, explaining, "When you have the friendship book with Allison, it makes me feel left out." Stephie makes half invitations to include you by saying things like, "You can come with us if you want to." But when you do, they still talk about stuff they did together or things you don't know about. When you again talk to Stephie about this, she says, "Well, Allison and I are good friends and we have secrets that we can't tell other people." Is Stephie acting like a bully?

Appendix 2

"What-If" Scenarios

"What-if" discussions concern real-life scenarios from which parents, teachers, and girls together can figure out solutions from the safety of emotional distance. Invite your daughter to come up with three ways she might act or three things she might say in a given situation, as well as two "I statements." Ask her to think of two adults she could talk to in each situation. Turn these scenarios into role-playing. They are also good to work through together, using the Four-Step plan.

Clubs*

Your seven-year-old friend Natalie creates a Kitties and Bunnies Club, wherein she brings a kitty or bunny to recess. Then the club members all make a house for it. Natalie makes you her assistant, which is like being co-president. A few days later, Miranda wants to join the club, but Natalie tells her she can't. You know the school rules say that anybody can play if she wants to. What do you wish you could do? What do you feel able to do?

Yo-yo friendships†

You love fourth grade and really like your new friend Tara. Tara is always nice and polite, and parents and teachers like her. She likes to decide what to

---

*Take a look at Maya's story, on page 79, for another scenario that involves clubs.
†Take a look at Grace's story, on page 105, for another scenario that involves yo-yo friendships.

do most of the time, but this is okay with you. While over for a playdate, Tara says she wants to play jump rope outside. You're not a great jump roper, but you're a great friend, so you go along. You play for a while, and then you tell Tara that you want to play school. While Tara agrees, once you get all the materials prepared, Tara says, "Actually I'm hungry, let's go get a snack." After snack, Tara suggests a different game, and you never end up playing school. This kind of thing happens all the time. What do you do, on the playdate or after?

Rumors, whispers, and secrets*

In art today, you hear Julia tell your close friend Emily not to be friends with you. Emily smiles and says it is a good idea. You can't speak because you're on the verge of tears and you don't want to cry in school. It is supposed to be a secret, but not only do you hear, your friend Samhita hears too. What can you do to feel better? How might you address this issue with the girls involved?

Powerful girls†

Today at lunch there was a table of four boys and four girls. You were sitting next to Sarah and Rebecca, with Jenna across from you. Emma had no seat and had to sit at another table. She flagged Rebecca to switch tables to sit with her. In less than a minute, Sarah and Jenna had followed suit and switched tables. You decided to switch too, to be with your friends. Three more girls sat quickly down, and one announced in triumph, "Another all-girls' table!" When Emma looked around at who was sitting at her table, she moved her lunch to the previously abandoned half-boy table, with Sarah, Rebecca, and Jenna in tow. You were left at the new table without any friends to sit next to. How are you feeling? What do you want to say? To whom? How do you want tomorrow to be different?

---

*Take a look at Carley's story, on page 138, for another scenario that involves rumors and whispers.
†Take a look at Natasha's story, on page 162, for another scenario that involves feeling excluded from a friendship group.

Appendix 3

Activities That Follow the Four Steps

Teacher Tips

Observe

Connect

Guide

Support to Act

Tips for Girls

Observe
1. Create a Journal, page 18
2. Follow Your Bliss, page 56
3. Feeling Powerful, page 230

Connect
1. What Is a Bully?, page 26
2. TV Time, page 60

Guide
1. Make a Mantra, page 64
2. Assert Yourself! page 88
3. Mismatched Barrettes, page 134
4. Whispers, Rumors, and Secrets, page 143
5. Gossip and Rumors, page 145
6. The Difference Between Gossiping and Checking-In, 158
7. Carry on the Kindness, page 192
8. Words Leave a Hole, page 241

Support to Act
1. Furthering Friendship Through Letter Writing, page 44
2. Friendship Notes, page 70
3. Take a Stand for Strangers, page 71
4. Developing "I Statements," page 91
5. When You Hear a Rumor About Yourself, page 123
6. Take a Stand for a Friend, page 155
7. Mirror, Mirror, page 160
8. Reflections on Talking Badly About Your Friend, page 173
9. If You Think You've Behaved Like a Mean Girl—Remember the Three Rs, page 207
10. Tokens of Friendships, page 228
11. A "Can" Can, page 250
12. Using What You Know, page 261

Appendix 3

Think, Share, Do . . .

Observe

Connect

Guide

Support to Act

Notes

1. J. S. Yoon, E. Barton, and J. Taiariol, "Relational Aggression in Middle School: Educational Implications of Developmental Research," *The Journal of Early Adolescence* 24 (2004): 303.
2. The Ophelia Project® www.opheliaproject.com, 718 Nevada Drive, Erie, PA 16505, Phone: (814) 456-5437.
3. N. R. Crick and J. K. Grotpeter, "Relational Aggression, Gender, and Social-Psychological Adjustment," *Child Development* 66 (1995): 710–722.
4. N. R. Crick, J. F. Casas, and M. Mosher, "Relational and Overt Aggression in Preschool." *Developmental Psychology* 33(4) (1997): 579–588.
5. N. R. Crick, "The Role of Overt Aggression, Relational Aggression, and Prosocial Behavior in the Prediction of Children's Future Social Adjustment." *Child Development* 67(5) (1996): 2317–2327.
6. L. Martocci, "Relational Aggression: The Social Destruction of Self Narratives." Paper presented at the annual meeting of the American Sociological Association, Hilton San Francisco & Renaissance Parc 55 Hotel, San Francisco, CA (2004).
7. N. R. Crick and J. K. Grotpeter, "Relational Aggression, Gender, and Social-Psychological Adjustment," *Child Development* 66 (1995): 710–762.
8. L. Martocci, "Relational Aggression: The Social Destruction of Self Narratives." Paper presented at the annual meeting of the American Sociological

Association, Hilton San Francisco & Renaissance Parc 55 Hotel, San Francisco, CA (2004).

9. Peggy Patten, "Pathways Project: An interview with Gary Ladd." *Parent News* [Online], 5(4). Available: http://npin.org/pnews/1999/pnew799/int799c.html [2000, May 14] (1999).

Index

Index

Index

Index

Index